HOTSPOTS

TURKEY
AEGEAN COAST

Çeşme, Kuşadası, Altınkum, Bodrum, Gümbet, The Bodrum Peninsula

Written by Lindsay Bennett; updated by Sean Sheehan
Original photography by Thomas Cook Publishing

Published by Thomas Cook Publishing
A division of Thomas Cook Tour Operations Limited.
Company registration no. 1450464 England
The Thomas Cook Business Park, Unit 9, Coningsby Road,
Peterborough PE3 8SB, United Kingdom
Email: books@thomascook.com, Tel: + 44 (0)1733 416477
www.thomascookpublishing.com

Produced by Cambridge Publishing Management Limited
Burr Elm Court, Main Street, Caldecote CB23 7NU

ISBN: 978-1-84157-862-0

Project Editor: Diane Ashmore
Production/DTP Editor: Steven Collins

Printed and bound in Spain by GraphyCems

CONTENTS

WHAT'S IN YOUR GUIDEBOOK?

Independent authors Impartial, up-to-date information from our travel experts who meticulously source local knowledge.

Experience Thomas Cook's 165 years in the travel industry and guidebook publishing enriches every word with expertise you can trust.

Travel know-how Contributions by thousands of staff around the globe, each one living and breathing travel.

Editors Travel-publishing professionals, pulling everything together to craft a perfect blend of words, pictures, maps and design.

You, the traveller We deliver a practical, no-nonsense approach to information, geared to how you really use it.

Lounging by the sea and soaking up the Turkish sun

INTRODUCTION

Getting to know Turkey's Aegean coast

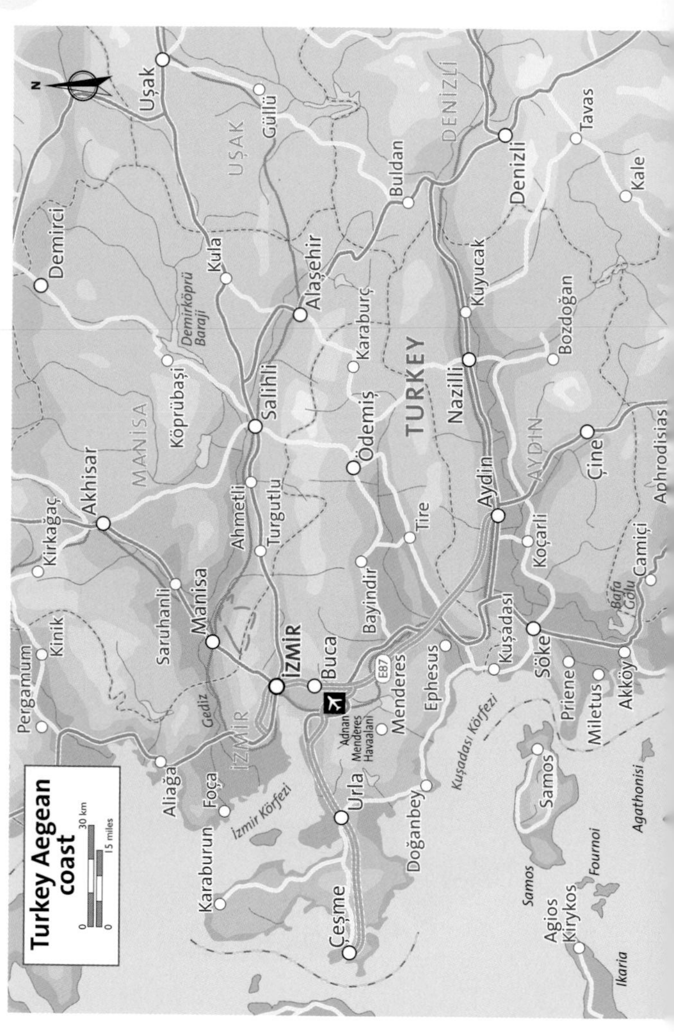
Turkey Aegean coast
0
30 km
0
15 miles
N
Uşak
Güllü
UŞAK
DENİZLİ
Tavas
Denizli
Kale
Buldan
Demirci
Kula
Demirköprü Baraji
Alaşehir
Kuyucak
Bozdoğan
Karaburç
TURKEY
Köprübaşi
MANİSA
Salihli
Ödemiş
Nazilli
Akhisar
Ahmetli
Turgutlu
Tire
Aydin
AYDIN
Çine
Aphrodisias
Kirkağaç
Koçarli
Camiçi
Bafa Gölü
Manisa
Saruhanli
Bayindir
Kuşadasi
Söke
Kinik
Pergamum
İZMİR
Buca
E87
Ephesus
Menderes
Adnan Menderes Havaalani
Priene
Miletus
Akköy
Gediz
Aliağa
Foça
Urla
Doğanbey
Kuşadası Körfezi
Samos
Agathonisi
İzmir Körfezi
Karaburun
Çeşme
Samos
Fournoi
Agios Kirykos
Ikaria

Aegean Sea
Leros
Kalymnos
Kos
Dodecanese
Astypalaia
Syrna
Nisyros
Tilos
Gümbet
Turgut Reis
Bodrum
Bodrum-Milas
Gökova Körfezi
Ören
Gökova
MUĞLA
Marmaris
Ortaca
Fethiye
Fethiye Körfezi
Altınkum
Datça
Emecik
Symi
Rhodes Town
Lindos
Rhodes
Monolithos
Chalki
Steno Karpathou
Karpathos
Diafani
Mediterranean Sea
Turkey Aegean

City
Large Town
Small Town
Motorway
Main Road
Minor Road
Airport
Railway

Getting to know Turkey's Aegean coast

What is your idea of the perfect holiday destination? Long, hot, sunny days, with beautiful sandy beaches? Crystal-clear seas and friendly people? Lots to see and do, but no rush to do anything? Then Turkey's Aegean coast – a touch of spice but with a few touches of home – is the place for you, whether you enjoy 'buzzing' nightlife or a quiet evening with just the buzzing of the cicadas.

A LAND RICH IN HISTORY

'Where East and West meet' or 'The Crossroads of History' are just two ways to describe this land. Turkey stretches from the Aegean Sea in the west into the Middle East and Asia in the east, and it has been used as a land bridge for hundreds of generations. Persians, Greeks, Romans, Byzantines and Ottomans all feature strongly in its long history and have left fascinating legacies for today's holidaymakers to explore.

VARIED NATURAL BEAUTY

Not a history buff? No worries! Turkey has much more to offer. The sheer beauty of the landscapes would be enough to draw the crowds, but here you can do more than simply gaze in awe. A whole fleet of boats cruises just offshore, jeep safaris navigate through forests, river beds and mountain passes, hiking trails point the way to panoramic vistas and you can pilot a jet ski or kayak to explore the coastal shallows.

If this all sounds too energetic, there is plenty of opportunity to bronze on the beach and dip your toes in the azure shallows with a beach bar just on the doorstep for that cooling drink – or you can head to a Turkish bath for a little pampering.

EVENING ENTERTAINMENT

Nightlife is varied here: the coast's larger towns offer some of the most raucous nightlife of any holiday destination in Europe – great foam parties and fishbowl cocktails – while smaller resorts are the perfect locations for romantic meals and moonlit strolls on the beach.

FASCINATING COASTLINE

The Aegean is Turkey's most westerly strip of land and the country's most beautiful and varied coastline. A couple of long peninsulas push out towards Greece, and many islands and islets sit just offshore. Tiny coves contrast with long swathes of sand that have helped this region to become Turkey's most developed tourist area. Kuşadası and the smaller resorts of Altınkum and Gümbet offer sheer energetic holiday fun, while Bodrum still has something of an enigmatic sophistication and Çeşme is a windsurfer's paradise.

The brush strokes of history can be seen on every corner, and this region has perhaps the greatest concentration of major ancient sites in Turkey. One of the most famous of these is Ephesus, unique in the Eastern Mediterranean, and the most visited attraction in the country.

AN ANCIENT WAY OF LIFE

Traditional lifestyles have all but disappeared on the coastal strip, but if you head just a little way inland you will discover it is a different matter. You will soon find yourself among farmers and their families. Here, the seasons pass with a riot of colour, with golden grain in the spring, bright yellow sunflowers in summer and snowy white cotton in the early autumn.

THE BEST OF TURKEY'S AEGEAN COAST

The Turkish Aegean offers a wealth of fantastic experiences that fill the hours from just after dawn until well after dusk. To get the most out of your trip, you need to travel backwards in time to the first millennium BC, then zip forward to the best in 21st-century fun. Here are some of the key attractions.

TOP 10 ATTRACTIONS

- **Barter for a bargain at the bazaar** Shopping is a performance on the Aegean coast – it is theatre, all designed to get you to part with your hard-earned cash.

- **Bodrum's castle** Explore the ancient underwater finds at Bodrum's castle. Marine archaeology was born here and this museum has some of the best finds in the world (pages 40–41).

- **Curetes Street at Ephesus** Walk in the footsteps of St Paul down Curetes Street at Ephesus, the most complete ancient city ever excavated in Asia Minor, and a place steeped in atmosphere (page 76).

- **Dip your toes in the water on a boat trip** There is nothing better to drain the stress from your body than to go on a simple *gület* (traditional wooden boat) journey, sailing around the Aegean coast to hidden coves.

- **Get foamed at Halikarnas disco** For a wild night out, it does not get more extreme than this (page 47).

- **Pamukkale, the 'cotton castle'** A strange natural phenomenon, with its glittering white pools of scallop-like hot springs that feature on a hillside (page 80).

- **Spa at Çeşme** Cleanse your body with a spa treatment at Çeşme. A new you? Well perhaps a revitalised you after a visit to one of these modern therapeutic centres (page 20).

- **The bars of Bodrum's old town** Chill out in the bars of Bodrum's old town. The Aegean's most sophisticated resort is perfect for a drink overlooking the harbour (page 46).

- **Visit another country – a day trip to Greece** Enjoy a few hours consuming *souvlaki* and *retsina*, just a little way off the Turkish coast on the Greek islands of Chios (see page 22) and Samos (see page 31).

- **Visit the ancient oracle at Didyma** Perhaps you will find out what this week's winning lottery numbers are (page 87)!

Hot springs at Pamukkale

SYMBOLS KEY

The following symbols are used throughout this book:

address telephone fax website address email

opening times important

The following symbols are used on the maps:

	information office		city
	post office		large town
	shopping		small town
	airport		POI (point of interest)
	hospital		motorway
	police station		main road
	bus station		minor road
	railway station		railway
	mosque		cathedral

1 numbers denote featured cafés, restaurants & evening venues

RESTAURANT CATEGORIES

The symbol after the name of each restaurant listed in this guide indicates the price of a typical three-course meal without drinks for one person:

£ budget price ££ mid-range price £££ most expensive

Sunset over Bodrum

RESORTS
Places under the sun

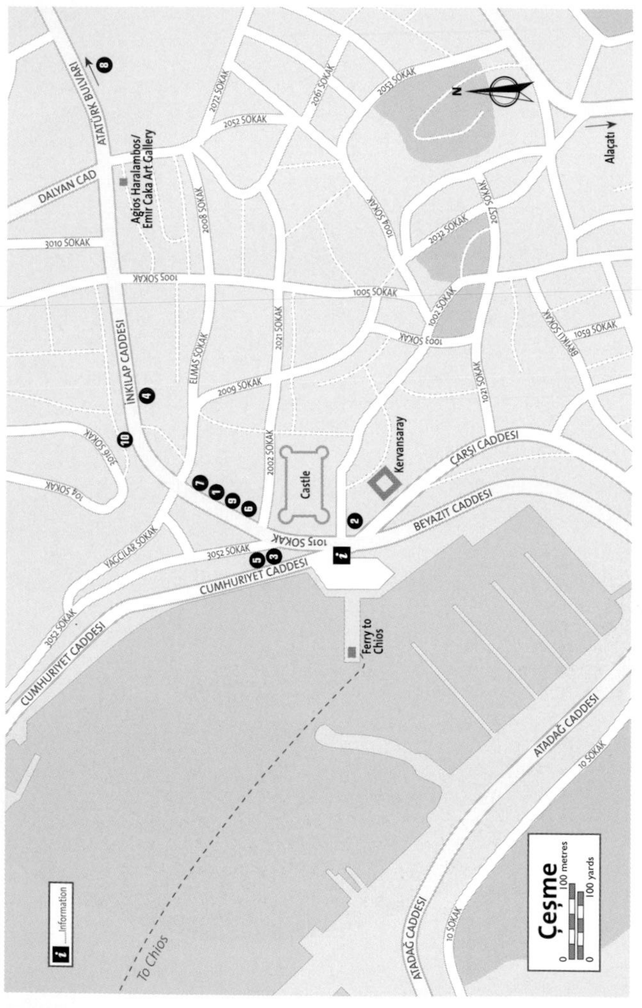
Çeşme
0 100 metres
0 100 yards
Information
To Chios
Ferry to Chios
Castle
Kervansaray
Agios Haralambos/ Emir Caka Art Gallery
Alaçati
ATATÜRK BULVARI
DALYAN CAD
İNKILAP CADDESI
CUMHURIYET CADDESI
BEYAZIT CADDESI
ÇARŞI CADDESI
ATADAĞ CADDESI
ELMAS SOKAK
YAGCILAR SOKAK
BRYIKLI SOKAK
3010 SOKAK
1005 SOKAK
2008 SOKAK
2052 SOKAK
2072 SOKAK
2061 SOKAK
2053 SOKAK
1004 SOKAK
2032 SOKAK
2057 SOKAK
1002 SOKAK
1003 SOKAK
1059 SOKAK
1021 SOKAK
2021 SOKAK
2009 SOKAK
2002 SOKAK
1015 SOKAK
3052 SOKAK
3016 SOKAK
104 SOKAK
10 SOKAK

Çeşme

Set on the very easternmost tip of the largest peninsula on the Aegean coast, Çeşme (pronounced Cheshmey) is a pretty town that has grown around a sturdy Genoese castle and Ottoman *kervansaray*. To the north and south there are numerous coves with small sandy bays and hills filled with fragrant orange groves.

The steady *imbat* winds blow across the peninsula all year round, making Çeşme cooler than many Turkish resorts. These winds are ideal for sailing and windsurfing – so much so that the region plays host to several international windsurfing tournaments throughout the summer season.

Çeşme's other claim to fame is its mineral springs. These have been drawing people here for therapy and pleasure since Roman times.

The imbat *winds make windsurfing around Turkey great fun*

Today its best hotels have high-class spa facilities, but you can still join the locals for free at public hot springs around the town.

Unusually for Turkey, Çeşme is a little short of ancient remains, but you are only a day trip away from several important archaeological sites.

HISTORY

Before the rise of İzmir (see page 71), Çeşme was the region's major port, and the end of the Silk Road for the camel caravans that crossed central Asia and the Middle East. From here the goods were taken by ship to the cities of the Mediterranean.

The Byzantines gave the town to the Genoese in the 14th century when they could not control the area. It was captured by the Ottomans in the 16th century but continued to have a large Greek Orthodox Christian (old Byzantine) population.

The Greek and Turkish communities lived together in relative peace until the Turkish Republic was founded in the 1920s. The Greek and Turkish governments decided to swap their two communities, so the Greeks here had to resettle on the Greek mainland and Turks born on Greek soil had to move across the Aegean to Turkey.

Today, Çeşme and its surrounding peninsula still have many reminders of Greek life, including distinctive architecture and abandoned churches dotting the hillsides.

BEACHES

Altınkum Beach

Çeşme's 'Golden Beach' offers several long, unspoilt golden sand bays that rival Ilıca as the best in the northern Aegean. There is far less development here but still a selection of cafés for refreshment.

ⓐ 9 km (5 miles) south of the town; there are regular *dolmuş* services from the bus station at Çeşme

Ayayorgi Beach

A secluded bay hidden among fragrant orange groves. There is no sand here, which is not ideal for young children. Instead you enter the sea via cement lidos. The waters here are exceptionally clear, so if you like snorkelling it is ideal. You can also rent kayaks and paddleboats to explore the rocky shoreline.

ⓐ 3 km (2 miles) north of Çeşme; there is no public transport, so you will need to take a taxi or hire a car

Ilıca

The primary beach area of Ilıca (Uluja) and the adjoining bay of Şifne (Shifni) have long, fine strands that are some of the best in the Aegean. The warm shallows of Şifne extend over 100 m (109 yds) out into the water. The Romans used to come here to enjoy the therapeutic springs, and today there are some excellent international five-star hotels here, offering a luxury that is not always available in the other major resorts.

ⓐ 2 km (1 mile) from Çeşme

White sand beaches stretch far along the coastline

Pırlanta Beach

Pirlanta, or 'Diamond Beach', is named after the brilliant, almost white sand that twinkles in the sunshine (sunglasses are advised).

ⓐ Closer to the town, by a couple of kilometres (a mile or so), than Altınkum

Tekke Beach

The town beach is not the best one around the resort, but it is the perfect place to cool down after a morning's shopping.

ⓐ Just north of the port in Çeşme

THINGS TO SEE & DO

Agios Haralambos

The large 19th-century Greek church of Agios Haralambos lay empty for many years after the exchange of populations in the 1920s, but today the plain, fortress-like building has been restored and reopened as the Emir Caka Art Gallery. It is the region's main cultural and art centre and offers a range of exhibitions throughout the summer.

ⓐ İnkilap Caddesi ⓑ 09.00–13.00 & 16.00–20.00 ⓘ Admission free

Boat trips

There are boat trips to isolated beaches and coves all around the peninsula, but one of the most popular is a visit out to Donkey Island. As the name suggests, it is inhabited by numerous donkeys that live wild. They were originally left here when the farmers abandoned the island and moved to the mainland. The donkeys thrived and the island has now been classified as a national park.

Castle

When the Genoese took control of the area in the 14th century they built the original fortress on the hillside overlooking the port. In the 16th century the castle was extended by the Ottomans, but it was destroyed during the wars with Venice in the 17th century. It was rebuilt

SHOPPING

İnkilap Caddesi, Çeşme's main street, is the centre for shopping and nightlife. There is a full range of souvenir shops here, from inexpensive to pricey, and it is traffic free, so you can stroll to your heart's content – that is, if the shopkeepers do not grab your attention.

One unique souvenir to look out for here is food flavoured with mastic (*sakız* in Turkish). The Çeşme peninsula is the only place in Turkey where this aromatic resin is harvested. The Ottomans used it as a breath freshener and flavouring. Local growers produce mastic jam, mastic ice cream and also mastic *rakı* (a strong spirit similar to vodka) by infusing the resin in the alcohol.

but lost its strategic value after 1833. It now houses the Çeşme Archaeological Museum with a small but interesting collection of armaments and finds from the area, including some from Erythrai.
ⓐ On the seafront ⓛ 08.30–17.30 May–Oct; 08.30–12.30 & 13.30–17.30 Nov–Apr; closed Mon ⓘ Admission charge

Club Mistral

This company, based in Germany, has wind- and kitesurfing training centres across the globe, with English-speaking instructors.
ⓐ Alaçatı, near Çeşme ⓣ 0232 716 9747 ⓦ www.club-mistral.com

Diving

Diving is taking off in the area. **Dolphin Land** (ⓐ Dalyankoy Limanı ⓣ 0232 435 7069 ⓦ www.divecesme.com) offers PADI training and accompanied dives for both beginners and qualified divers and has over 20 dive sites around the peninsula.

Kervansaray or Caravanserai

The 16th-century *kervansaray* – a place where the camel trains could rest along the silk route – of Öküz Mehmet Pasa was a gift from Sultan

Süleyman the Magnificent. It was built to provide accommodation for travellers taking the journey across to Chios and is still a hotel today, although it has been totally renovated. Wander into the cool courtyard and maybe have some tea while you enjoy the architecture.
ⓐ Beyazıt Caddesi ⓛ 24 hours ⓘ Admission free

Kitesurfing

The centre of Turkish kitesurfing is based at Pırlanta beach which benefits from the prevailing Aegean winds and has hosted national and international championships. The **kitesurfing school** (ⓐ Pırlanta Plaji Çiftlik Köy ⓣ 0532 244 8348 ⓦ www.kitesurfbeach.com) at the beach is the best in Turkey and you can take beginners' courses or rent equipment.

Tour of the Drinking Fountains

The word Çeşme means 'drinking fountain' in Turkish and the name is derived from the more than 40 fountains and ornate public water sources that once decorated the town. Today there are still over a dozen Seljuk and Ottoman fountains in the streets of the old town – you can sometimes pick up a simple map from the tourist office (ⓐ İskele Meydanı 8 – in the main square of the town ⓣ 0232 712 6653) that leads you to them.

Windsurfing

Active-Surf Centre This is the place to go for instruction and board rental. You can start from scratch or take one-to-one improver courses. There is a wide range of boards and sails, and the centre has a beach volleyball field for relaxation.
ⓐ Alaçatı Beach ⓣ 0232 716 6383 ⓦ www.active-surf.com

SPAS & TURKISH BATHS

Çeşme is famous for its natural hot springs, renowned since antiquity for their health-giving properties. The water temperature is 55°C (131°F) and contains sodium chloride, magnesium sulphate and calcium bicarbonate. The mineral-rich water is relaxing and said to cure various ailments.

Belediye Hamamı A genuine old bathhouse that offers mixed sessions several times per week.
Ⓐ Near the *kervansaray* Ⓛ 08.00–22.00

The Spavit Center This place offers medical therapies and a full range of relaxing and well-being treatments such as reflexology, facials and massage. There is also a sports centre, hot mineral springs and a *hamam*.
Ⓐ Süzer Paradise Limanı Mevkii, Çark Plajı, right on the beach
Ⓣ 0232 716 9777 Ⓔ spavit@suzerparadise.com

Thermalife Natural Spa This 7,869 sq m (25,800 sq ft) spa centre includes an indoor seawater pool, sauna, steam room, thalassotherapy jet and affusion showers, physiotherapy area, fitness centre and beauty salon. Treatments include hydrating moss or mud body wrap, and pressotherapy, a rejuvenating full-body lymphatic drainage massage, plus a full range of aromatherapy and massage treatments to reduce stress, eliminate toxins and increase metabolism. If you don't want a treatment, you can just take a swim in the natural thermal pools. This is the most luxurious place for a swim, but it is also the most expensive.
Ⓐ Sheraton Çeşme Hotel Resort & Spa, Şifne Caddesi 35, Ilıca
Ⓣ 0232 723 1240 Ⓦ www.starwood.com Ⓛ 09.00–20.00

Yıldız The Yıldız peninsula thermal spring is popular with local families. The temperature of the water reaches 60°C (140°F), but it emerges into cooler seawater already in the rocky natural pool.
Ⓐ West of Ilıca town Ⓘ Admission free Ⓛ 09.00–18.00

EXCURSIONS

Alaçatı

Alaçatı is a wonderful old town with some excellent, 19th-century Greek mansions surrounded by a verdant landscape of orange and olive groves plus the only mastic orchards in Turkey.

A collection of old windmills lines the hillside, and some have been converted into good restaurants and cafés. They do not work, but their

presence gives an indication of the strength of the winds that blow down the Aegean across the peninsula. Today these year-round high winds (and shallow water) help to make the beach at Alaçatı one of the top three windsurfing destinations in the world. There are lots of small shops in Calcatı, and Agrilia is the best of the many restaurants (75 Kemalpasa Cad). ⓐ Located 9 km (6 miles) southeast of Çeşme; the beach is 4 km (2½ miles) from town

Ertürk Agency organises a range of activities and trips on the surrounding Çeşme peninsula. ⓐ Beyazıt Caddesi 7 ⓣ 0232 712 6768

Chios (Hios)

You will find the Greek island of Chios delightfully free of visitors because it is one of the least 'touristy' islands in the Aegean. The capital of the island, Chios Town, is one of the least attractive towns in the Greek Aegean, but it has a fine castle and archaeological museum. It is best to rent a car or agree a rate with a taxi to tour the island's other attractions.

Chios has made a living out of mastic for centuries, and the mastic villages (*mastihohoria*) inland boast some grand Genoese mansions built in the 14th and 15th centuries, set among a glorious verdant countryside. Pyrgi village is unique because of its distinctive decoration. The walls of all the houses are covered with black and white geometric patterns called *xysta*. It is also worth visiting Nea Moni, one of the most beautiful religious sites in the Aegean. Founded in 1049, the church has some exceptional Byzantine mosaics. There are daily trips (weather permitting) from the harbour, and commercial ferries from the new harbour.

Erythrai

The Çeşme peninsula has the least amount of ancient remains along the Aegean coast, but there is one small site. Erythrai was the site of a renowned Sybil, or prophetess, and also had a temple containing a statue of Hercules.

Most of the stone has been recycled for later buildings, so there is not much to see. Some sections of what must have been a vast outer wall are still standing, and there is a Roman villa and a Hellenistic (late Greek) mosaic floor. Statues, jewellery and other finds from the city are on show in the Archaeological Museum at İzmir (see page 71).

Because the area has been declared a national heritage site by the Turkish authorities, the modern village of Ildırı on the site cannot be expanded and is semi-abandoned. The Acropolis at the top of the site offers wonderful views across the small islands of the Aegean, especially at sunset.
ⓐ 20 km (12 miles) northeast of Çeşme

TAKING A BREAK

Bizе Bize £ ❶ Authentic, inexpensive Turkish snacks at this tiny establishment that specialises in *İskender* and *döner kepabs*. A great place for hungry tums at lunchtime or during a shopping trip.
ⓐ İnkılap Caddesi 6 ⓛ 08.00–01.00

Kale Lokantası £ ❷ One of the best places in the Aegean to try good home-cooked Turkish dishes in an authentic *lokanta*. It has a rustic interior but the food is excellent, and great value for money. There is no menu, just a small choice of traditional dishes (whatever is fresh and in season). They also do a tasty *döner kepab*. Not surprisingly, Kale gets very busy with locals and you will not go wrong if you follow their lead.
ⓐ Kervansaray yanı 11, Çarşı Caddesi ⓣ 0232 712 0519 ⓛ 09.00–24.00

Özsüt £ ❸ In front of the Ridvan Otel and facing the town square, come here to sit and enjoy flavoured coffees, cakes, tarts, pastries, ice cream and sundaes. ⓐ Cumhuriyet Meydanı ⓣ 0232 712 6336
ⓛ 07.30–24.00

Rumeli Pastanesi £ ❹ Turks flock to this shop for the very best homemade ice-cream, including a mastic flavour which is unique to this area. It's a good option to finish your meal. ⓐ İnkılap Caddesi 44
ⓛ 09.00–24.00

Beyaz Köse ££ ❺ Elegant restaurant in the centre of town. The menu is a wide-ranging one, but the fish is your best bet. Tables indoors and outside on the corner of the square. ⓐ 16 Eylül Mah ⓣ 0232 712 7989 ⓛ 07.00–02.00

Restoran Patika ££–£££ ❻ A converted town house now makes a pretty restaurant with a vast menu and prices to suit every pocket. There's live music every evening in the summer. ⓐ Cumhuriyet Meydani (left of the Belediye or Town Hall) ⓣ 0232 712 6357 ⓛ 11.00–24.00

Restoran İmren £££ ❼ This is a place to treat yourself to something a little more upscale with slightly more formal service but still with that classic Turkish welcome. The best restaurant in town. ⓐ İnkılap Caddesi 6 ⓣ 0232 712 7620 ⓛ 08.30–19.30

AFTER DARK

Felix Roof Bar ❽ At the top of the 5-star Sheraton Hotel, this bar is one of the most sophisticated and expensive in the northern Aegean. The surroundings are luxurious and offer long-range views across the bay. There's live music nightly. ⓐ Sheraton Çeşme Hotel, Şifne Caddesi 35, Ilıca ⓣ 0232 723 1240 ⓛ 16.00–02.00

Wine Plaza ❾ This is the latest hip place to be in Çeşme, contained in an old Greek mansion that has been beautifully transformed into a sophisticated wine bar. The food on offer is Italian style but this is more of an after-dinner spot. Enjoy a glass of wine out on the terrace – there's a good range of Turkish options for you to try – or come after 22.30 Wed–Sat to enjoy live music. ⓐ İnkılap Caddesi 27 ⓣ 0232 712 095 ⓛ 12.00–03.00

Kuşadası

Kuşadası (pronounced Kushadaser) is a vast and seemingly ever-expanding holiday town. It is probably Turkey's most versatile resort, with a huge selection of hotels, apartments, restaurants and bars for package tourists, one of the largest marinas along the coast for the yachting crowd and a huge cruise port for passengers on the Aegean tour who disembark in the morning to visit Ephesus (see page 75) and get whisked away to their next port of call in Greece – usually sailing before nightfall.

The heart of Kuşadası is a tiny old town with a maze of narrow alleyways planned and built during Ottoman times. You will find some of the best shopping and nightlife in Turkey here, with top-quality jewellery, leather and carpet shops tempting the cruise-ship crowd, mass-produced designer fakes, plus a huge selection of bars and clubs with a young, boisterous and mainly British crowd.

Today 'holidayland' stretches over several kilometres of coastline. It cannot be described as attractive, with the hills covered with a jungle of white-painted concrete, but for 'party central' look no further.

For more information contact the tourist office ⓐ Liman Caddesi 13 across from the port entrance ⓣ 0256 614 1103

HISTORY

No one knows exactly when the site was first settled, but the nearby ancient city of Panionian was the annual meeting place of the Ionian League in the first millennium BC. When the port of Ephesus dried up in the 6th and 7th centuries, Kuşadası took over and became an important trade centre run by Venetian and Genoese merchants. They built the fortress to guard the port.

In the 16th century the Ottomans arrived and Kuşadası was reinvented by Öküz Mehmet Paşa, grand vizier to a couple of Ottoman sultans. He built the *kervansaray*, expanded the fortress and chose to call the town Kuşadası, or 'Bird Island', a name taken from the tiny island situated just offshore.

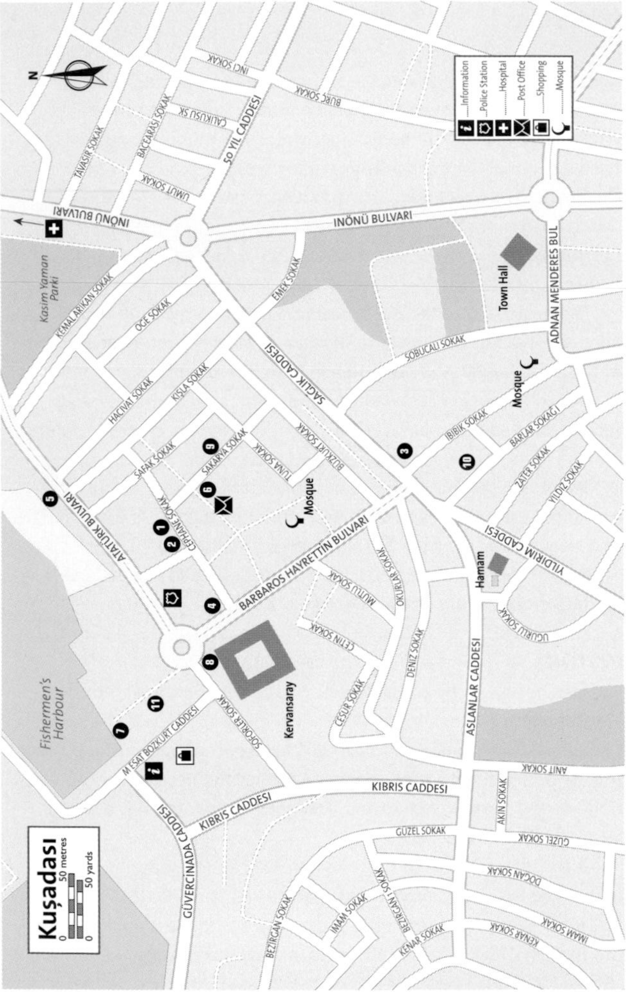

Kuşadası
0 50 metres
0 50 yards

Information
Police Station
Hospital
Post Office
Shopping
Mosque

Fishermen's Harbour
Kasim Yaman Parki
Kervansaray
Town Hall
Hamam
Mosque
Mosque

INÖNÜ BULVARI
50 YIL CADDESI
INCI SOKAK
BURÇ SOKAK
ÇALIKUŞU SK
BACEARASI SOKAK
TAVASIR SOKAK
UMUT SOKAK
KEMAL ARIKAN SOKAK
OGE SOKAK
EMEK SOKAK
SAĞLIK CADDESI
HACIVAT SOKAK
KIŞLA SOKAK
SÖBUCALI SOKAK
ADNAN MENDERES BUL
IBIBIK SOKAK
BARLAR SOKAĞI
ZATER SOKAK
YILDIZ SOKAK
YILDIRIM CADDESI
ŞAFAK SOKAK
SAKARYA SOKAK
TUNA SOKAK
BOZKURT SOKAK
CEPHANE SOKAK
ATATÜRK BULVARI
BARBAROS HAYRETTIN BULVARI
MUTLU SOKAK
OKURLAR SOKAK
ÇETIN SOKAK
UĞURLU SOKAK
DENIZ SOKAK
CESUR SOKAK
ASLANLAR CADDESI
SOFORLER SOKAK
M ESAT BOZKURT CADDESI
KIBRIS CADDESI
ANIT SOKAK
AKIN SOKAK
GÜZEL SOKAK
DOĞAN SOKAK
GÜVERCINADA CADDESI
BEZIRGAN SOKAK
IMAM SOKAK
BEZIRGAN 1 SOKAK
KENAR SOKAK

BEACHES

Barbaros Beach

Barbaros is popular with local families and is usually only packed at weekends. A good, sandy stretch, it is quieter than Ladies Beach, with fewer cafés and bars.

ⓐ Only five minutes south of Ladies Beach on foot

Kuştur Beach

Kuştur is a little over 1 km (just over half a mile) of fine sand that has been developed since the 1990s. Because it is a new, pre-planned area, there is an excellent range of cafés and restaurants plus a good choice of watersports. The sea often gets rougher in the afternoon as the winds down the Aegean get stronger.

ⓐ 6 km (4 miles) north of Kuşadası

Ladies Beach

Kuşadası's most famous beach, this kilometre-long sandy stretch is the heart and soul of holiday fun. Backed by hotels with an excellent range of bars and eateries close by, it also has a full range of facilities, including a good range of watersports. This is the place to be for the young crowd; it does get very busy in high season, so arrive early to get a sunbed.

ⓐ A couple of kilometres (1 mile) south of the town centre

Long Beach

As the name suggests, Long Beach is the longest in the Kuşadası region, at 6 km (4 miles). It is now backed by a number of hotels and pensions, so you'll find good watersports at **Aqualand Waterpark**, and a range of cafés, bars and restaurants.

ⓐ South of the town

Pamucak Beach

This long, wide beach is an excellent stretch of sand and contains the **Aquafantasy Waterpark**. The southern end is developed, with some large

hotel complexes, but you can still escape the crowds if you walk along towards where the River Menderes meets the sea. Some facilities, but not as organised as Ladies Beach.
ⓐ 10 km (6 miles) north of the town

Snake Beach

Just to the left of Pigeon Island, Snake Beach covers two sides of a small peninsula. There are sunbeds and umbrellas and a couple of cafés for snacks, but no watersports.
ⓐ 10 minutes' walk from the town centre

THINGS TO SEE & DO

Adaland Waterpark

Some 10 ha (25 acres) of parkland with 20 rides, including Kamikaze, a 52 m (171 ft) drop, children's pool, ring rides and water slides. The park also includes water disco, a bowling alley and beach volleyball. Bars serve alcohol as well as soft drinks.
ⓐ Çam Limanı, 5 km (3 miles) north of Kuşadası ⓣ 0256 618 1252
ⓦ www.adaland.com 🕒 10.00–18.00 May–June; 10.00–19.00 July–Aug; closed Nov–Apr

Aquafantasy Waterpark

The largest water park in Turkey, Aquafantasy has some of the highest energy rides, including the 'Castle' – three interloping slides of 120 m (400 ft) – and 'Proracer', the only head-down ride in Turkey with four lanes for slide racing. It also features a pool with ten different types of wave, plus 'Treasure Island', an area specifically for young children.
ⓐ Ephesus Beach, Pamucak ⓣ 0256 612 7237 🕒 10.00–18.00 (until 19.00 mid-June–early Sept) ❗ Admission charge

Aqualand

Some 70,000 sq m (76,580 sq yds) of pools, rides and slides, plus a range of watersports equipment on the beach.

ⓐ Sahil Siteleri, Long Beach ⓣ 0256 618 1252 ⓛ 09.00–18.00; longer in July–Aug; closed Nov–Apr

Diving

Aquaventure Diving Centre This centre offers several dive sites and courses at all levels. ⓐ Adjacent to Blue Sky Water Sports, at the Grand Blue Sky Resort ⓣ 0256 612 8330

Seahorse Diving Offers PADI training and guided dive tours for qualified visitors. ⓐ Klaus Murr. Adil Caylan, Deniz Güleç Sokak 1/A and at the Hotel Zinos ⓣ 0256 614 3561

Güvercin Adası

Bird Island was renamed Güvercin Adası, or 'Pigeon Island', and today it is connected to the mainland by a pedestrian causeway that acts as a dock for small excursion boats. The shady terraced area around the fortifications has relaxing tea gardens and cafés and offers lovely views at sunset and across the seafront and cruise port.

ⓐ On the waterfront ⓛ Castle 08.00–17.30 Tues–Sun; closed Mon
ⓘ Admission charge

Öküz Mehmet Paşa Kervansaray

Wander into the cool courtyard of this 16th-century *kervansaray* – a sort of guesthouse/hotel where you could also rest your animals – that has been welcoming guests for over 300 years. Today the architecture remains authentic although the rooms have all the mod cons. There is a good carpet shop here (expensive) and the hotel holds regular 'Turkish evenings' (see page 63).

ⓐ Atatürk Bul ⓣ 0256 614 4155 ⓛ 24 hours ⓘ Admission free, with charge for Turkish night

Spas & Turkish baths

Both the baths listed here offer mixed male and female sessions.

Belediye Hamamı ⓐ Sağlık Caddesi ⓣ 0256 614 1219 ⓛ 08.00–20.00
Kaleiçi Hamamı ⓐ Eylül Sokak 7 Kaleiçi ⓣ 0256 614 1292 ⓛ 08.00–20.00

SHOPPING

Kuşadası has the biggest range of shopping in the Aegean, with a great choice in all price ranges, but it also has some of the most persistent salesmen in the business.

You will find the upmarket shops clustered on the seafront (Atatürk Bul) and around the old *kervansaray*. These air-conditioned emporia stock huge silk carpets, Chanel, Prada and Dolce and Gabbana jewellery, plus the biggest diamonds you have ever seen. Quality does not come cheap, but you will pay less than for the genuine article at home.

Kuşadası is also famed for its designer rip-offs, some of them of very good quality. Whatever is in fashion at home, you will find a less expensive fake version here. Although the narrow streets have plenty of shops, you will find the greatest choice at the main bazaar. This is a very touristy market and the sales patter is constant, but you can pick up excellent bargains including watches, sunglasses, bags and clothing. The bazaar is also a great place to buy leather goods (bags, jackets and trousers) and to stock up on socks and underwear.

The Friday market (opposite the main bus station) is the place where the farmers of the region bring their crops for sale. It is a really bustling, atmospheric place.

In Kuşadası you will find lots of souvenirs priced in pounds, so do not change all your spending money into Turkish Lira.

Watersports

Blue Sky Water Sports Has an excellent beach-sports and watersports centre with jet skis, parasailing, water rides such as bananas, water-skis and sea kayaks. ⓐ The Grand Blue Sky Resort just north of Ladies Beach ⓣ 0256 613 1203 ⓛ 09.00–19.00

KoruMar Hotel A 5-star hotel 2 km (1 mile) north of the town with a full range of watersports, water rides and activities. ⓐ Gazi Begandi Mevkii ⓣ 0256 618 1530 ⓦ www.korumarhotel.com.tr ⓛ 09.00–19.00

There is a charge for non-guests for entrance to the beach, in addition to equipment rental

EXCURSIONS

Dilek National Park

A rocky finger of land pointing out into the Aegean, the Dilek peninsula is one of the largest remaining swathes of unspoilt pine forest left along the Aegean coast. Its strategic position close to the Greek island of Samos saved it from development because it was off limits to all but the Turkish military. Today, they still have a base at the western end, but the rest, now a national park, is a great place to come and get away from the crowds.

The small, sandy coves and crystal-clear waters are perfect for sunbathing, swimming and snorkelling. They line the northern shore and get quieter the further away you get from the ticket office – from İçmeler Köyü, the most crowded and with café and picnic tables, to Karasu Köyü, a pebble beach with views out to Samos.

Dilek is also a great place for walking and hiking (be prepared with water, snacks and proper clothing). The park protects several species of rare animals including, it is said, a small population of lynx (wild cats).

Dilek Park 30 km (19 miles) south of Kuşadası; take a *dolmuş* (bus) from Kuşadası to the first beach, but your own transport is more practical for touring the whole park 08.00–18.30 Admission charge

Samos

The Greek Island of Samos, located 3 km (2 miles) off the Turkish coastline just south of Kuşadası, has taken a back seat in Aegean history since its 'golden age' in the 6th century BC and today is known mostly for its vast pine forests. The capital, Samos Town, or Bathy, on the north coast, has a fine harbour-front promenade, but the smaller town of Pithagorio on the south coast makes a better excursion.

An ancient capital during the reign of the powerful ruler Polycrates in the 6th century BC (he had storyteller Aesop and mathematician Pythagoras in his court), Pithagorio has a picturesque harbour and ancient remains. In the hills above is perhaps the most amazing example of Polycrates' wealth and power. He funded the cutting of a tunnel over 1,000 m (1,094 yds) long through the hill to bring water to the capital. The Tunnel of Eupalinos can be explored, but it is not for the claustrophobic.

To the west, beyond the airport, are the remains of the Temple of Hera, or the Heraion. It would have been the largest in the world at the time, but it was never completed.

ⓐ Daily trips (weather permitting early and late in the season) take place from Kuşadası harbour. Departure at 08.30, return 18.45.
ⓣ 0256 614 1553 ⓦ www.azimtours.com

TAKING A BREAK

Avlu £ ❶ Always popular with local Turks, this traditional *lokanta* has no menu but serves a range of good, basic hearty food. Head into the kitchen to see what looks tasty, but try the succulent lamb stew with pilaf rice if you can. ⓐ Cephane Sokak, off Barbaros Hayrettin Caddesi (second turning before the post office) ⓣ 0256 614 7995 ⓛ 08.00–24.00

Öz Urfa £ ❷ Good, clean kepab place that has been in business for ages. Öz Urfa has the advantage that it is licensed, so you can get beer or wine with your meal. ⓐ Cephane Sokak 9 ⓣ 0252 614 6070 ⓛ 08.00–24.00

Panorama £ ❸ Fine for a late breakfast or light lunch and always relaxing for a coffee break; pleasant too at night. ⓐ Sağlik Caddesi 10 ⓣ 0256 612 0409 ⓛ 09.00–01.00

Paşa Restaurant £–££ ❹ This family-run restaurant has tables set out in the pretty courtyard of an old Greek mansion. The menu concentrates on standard *meze*, grills and kepabs, for which they have a good reputation, plus a small selection of seafood. ⓐ Cephane Sokak 21 ⓣ 0252 612 3133 ⓛ 11.00–24.00

Captain's House ££ ❺ A wonderful, renovated mansion houses this renowned fish restaurant and bar, which has an excellent reputation with locals and visitors looking for somewhere upmarket to eat. Lovely terrace. ⓐ Atatürk Bul 66 ⓣ 0256 612 1200 ◷ 11.00–02.00 ❶ Make reservations in high season

Erzincan ££ ❻ Down the Sokak by the side of the post office. The menu is aimed squarely at tourists: pizza, steak, kepab. ⓐ Bahar Sokak 4 ⓣ 0256 613 3442 ◷ 10.30–24.00

AFTER DARK

Kuşadası's nightlife is the loudest and most energetic in the Aegean and much of it is found in the old town, in the narrow streets bordered by Barbaros Hayrettin Caddesi and Sağlik Sokak. It is said that Kuşadası's Barlar Sokaği (walk up Barbaros Hayrettin Caddesi, turn right onto Sağlik Sokak, and then left under the arch) boasts more Irish pubs per square metre than Dublin. Although this must be an exaggeration, it tells you what to expect – lots of bars and discos competing for your money. Bar crawling seems to be the norm, but here are a few places you might want to try:

Çam ££ ❼ Overlooking the fishing port, it is not surprising that this restaurant serves a good range of excellent fresh seafood. The décor is basic, but the restaurant has a very good reputation. ⓐ Balıkçı Limanı ⓣ 0256 614 1051 ◷ 11.00–24.00

Club Caravanserail ❽ One of the best places in the Aegean to enjoy a Turkish night folklore show. The genuine Ottoman *kervansaray* sets the scene with its architecture, and the show takes place in the central courtyard. The food is of a reasonable quality and it is an entertaining evening. ⓐ Atatürk Bul 2 ⓣ 0256 614 4115 ❶ Performances nightly at 21.00 hours in peak season – drops to two or three times a week early or late in season

Ecstasy ❾ Kuşadası's major nightclub is a massive open-air arena that tends to stick mainly to the latest top 40 dance tunes. This is the venue where you can finish your evening after a few drinks in the bars earlier on. ⓐ Sakarya Sokak 10 ⓣ 0256 612 2208 ⓛ 21.00–04.00

Jimmy's Bar ❿ Long-standing Irish-style bar with energetic staff and loud music from the 1970s through to today. Jimmy's shows Premier League football matches on large-screen TVs so you will not miss too much soccer while you are relaxing. ⓐ Barlar Sokaği ⓣ 0256 612 1318 ⓛ 11.00–04.00

Kazım Usta ££ ⓫ The seafood here is excellent, and Turks also come for the extensive and delicious *meze* selection. ⓐ Balıkçı Limanı, on the harbour front ⓣ 0256 614 1226 ⓛ 12.00–24.00

Altınkum

Altınkum (pronounced Altunkum) has developed fast since the early 1980s. The long 'golden beach' that gives the resort its name is its claim to fame, and the three bays along the coastline have everything both children and adults need for holiday fun. This resort is a favourite with many UK tourists, with a range of 'roast beef dinner' restaurants and re-runs of favourite TV comedy shows or live football matches in the bars. As a result, hundreds of Britons have bought apartments here in the last few years. From here it is an easy excursion ride to the best the Aegean area has to offer. If you want a good beach resort with more than a few reminders of home, this is the place for you.

BEACHES

The busiest beach, **First Beach** sits directly in front of the heart of town and has access to most cafés, bars and a good range of watersports. It does get very crowded in high season. **Second Beach** is a little less developed, and for the most peace and quiet (just a couple of cafés and lots of free sand) head to **Third Beach** where you also have the best snorkelling.

THINGS TO SEE & DO

Boat trips

Most tour boats will take you on the 'five-island' tour, though few actually stop at any island. Swimming and snorkelling is from the boat.

EXCURSIONS

Bodrum by boat

There is a daily ferry to Bodrum (see page 39) during the summer, where you can sample a little Turkish sophistication.

Didyma

The ancient temple site at Didyma (see page 87) is only 5 km (3 miles) north of the resort at the village of Didim.

TAKING A BREAK

Janibo's ££ English-owned restaurant with a huge garden that serves a genuine English breakfast and UK favourites throughout the day, including scones and cream and trifle. There are sports channels on the big screen and a free pool. ⓐ Karakol Caddesi No 4 ⓣ 0256 813 4302 ⓛ 07.00–02.00

Pinocchio's ££ With a dining terrace on the seafront on First Beach, Pinocchio's has a great setting. The menu is Turkish/English (including traditional Sunday lunch and freshly baked bread and cakes) with a trained management team and an attention to detail that others do not always have. Live entertainment. ⓐ Yalı Caddesi 71, First Beach ⓣ 0256 813 1215 ⓛ 08.00–02.00

A Touch of Class ££ An unassuming restaurant that has been in business since the early 1990s while its more glamorous neighbours have come and gone, A Touch of Class offers good Turkish food and adds entertainment such as karaoke and Turkish nights into the mix. There is a good-value set meal. ⓐ Yalı Caddesi Goçler Mevkii 129 ⓣ 0256 813 1168 ⓛ 07.00–24.00

AFTER DARK

Alo 24 £ The best place in town for an inexpensive lunch or snacks throughout the day – Alo 24 turns out tons of *pide* and *döner kepabs*. It is a really inexpensive place for children to fill up after an action-packed day on the beach. ⓐ Atatürk Bul, opposite GIMA Supermarket ⓛ 07.00–23.00

British Pub Opened in 1997, British Pub does exactly what it says on the tin and has a loyal band of annual regulars. ⓐ Yali Caddesi 123 ⓛ 08.00–03.00

Ege Bar A long-standing favourite for the last few years, Ege has entertaining staff and dancers, but is also a great place to chill in the early evenings. ⓐ Dolphin Square ⓛ 11.00–03.00

Medusa Nightclub The largest venue and only real club in Altınkum has great chart and Turkish pop music. It is open air, so you can enjoy the stars while you dance. You may need to queue to get in during peak season. ⓐ Yalı Konağı Caddesi ⓛ 21.00–04.00 June–early Sept ⓘ Admission charge includes first drink

Altınkum has beautiful, sandy beaches

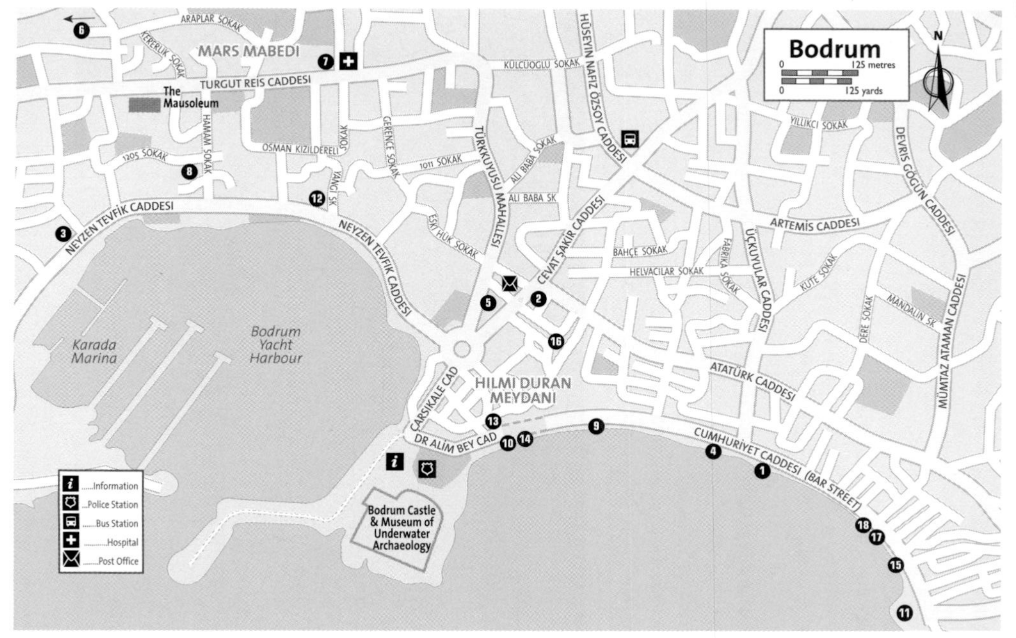
Bodrum
0 125 metres
0 125 yards
N
MARS MABEDI
ARAPLAR SOKAK
KERERLIK SOKAK
TURGUT REIS CADDESI
The Mausoleum
HAMAM SOKAK
1205 SOKAK
OSMAN KIZILDERELI SOKAK
GERENCE SOKAK
YANGI SK
1011 SOKAK
KULCUOGLU SOKAK
HÜSEYIN NAFIZ ÖZSOY CADDESI
TÜRKKUYUSU MAHALLESI
ALI BABA SOKAK
ALI BABA SK
CEVAT ŞAKIR CADDESI
ESKI HUK SOKAK
NEYZEN TEVFIK CADDESI
BAHÇE SOKAK
HELVACILAR SOKAK
FABRIKA SOKAK
ÜÇKUYULAR CADDESI
ARTEMIS CADDESI
KUTE SOKAK
YILLIKCI SOKAK
DEVRIS GÖGÜN CADDESI
DERE SOKAK
MANDALIN SK
MÜMTAZ ATAMAN CADDESI
ATATÜRK CADDESI
Karada Marina
Bodrum Yacht Harbour
CARSIKALE CAD
HILMI DURAN MEYDANI
DR ALIM BEY CAD
CUMHURIYET CADDESI (BAR STREET)
Bodrum Castle & Museum of Underwater Archaeology
Information
Police Station
Bus Station
Hospital
Post Office

Bodrum

Turkey's oldest tourist resort, the fishing community of Bodrum was adopted by the Turkish artistic community in the 1920s. It continues to attract an upmarket Turkish clientele who head out of İstanbul or Ankara during the summer. Bodrum was discovered by European holidaymakers in the 1980s, but refused to bow to the pressure to 'build 'em high and build 'em quick' that has spoilt some resorts, and passed laws to restrict building size and design. It has retained its authentic character and is perhaps the prettiest resort in the Aegean and one of the most attractive in Turkey.

The town has many attractions and caters to many different types of visitor. It is popular with the yachting crowd, who moor up in the large harbour and frequent the waterfront bars and restaurants. It is a great place to be young and fashionable, rivalling the Mediterranean hot spots

Bodrum castle overlooking the marina

of Ibiza in Spain and Mykonos in Greece. Bodrum also has the best range of shopping and dining in the Aegean, with something good to suit every pocket.

Staying in Bodrum will not suit everyone, however. Most town hotels are small and traditional rather than large 'resort' establishments with lots of activities. Also, one thing that the resort lacks is a good beach. The town beach is narrow, crowded and not very attractive. Families and 'bronzers' would be better making a base at one of Bodrum's close satellite resorts such as Gümbet (see page 49) or Bitez (see page 55). From both these places you can take a short *dolmuş* trip into Bodrum – in summer these operate almost 24 hours a day – to sample its sophisticated and cosmopolitan atmosphere.

HISTORY

The town was once the ancient city of Halicarnassus, home to the Carian people. The most famous Carian ruler, King Mausolus (*c.* 377–353 BC), built himself a monumental tomb known as the Mausoleum that became one of the 'seven wonders of the ancient world'. The Knights of St John made Bodrum their home after they were ousted from Jerusalem, but they had to leave when the Ottomans arrived in the area in the 14th century.

THINGS TO SEE & DO

Birdwatching

The Su Hotel offers guided walks in the countryside around Bodrum and guided birdwatching throughout the year.

ⓐ Turgut Reis Caddesi 1202 ⓣ 0252 316 6906 ⓘ Admission charge; pre-booking essential

Castle of St Peter (the Petronium) or Bodrum Castle

This is one of the finest and most complete castles in Turkey, built by the crusading Knights of St John in 1408. The building alone, with its dungeon and towers, would make it worth a visit, but the castle is also

SHOPPING

Bodrum has probably the best range of shopping in the Aegean. Hip and chic boutiques sit side by side with antique shops, genuine designer names try to attract the yachting set, while market stalls sell rip-offs at a fraction of the price.

Wandering along the streets of the old town – explore the narrow alleyways off **Cumhuriyet Caddesi** and **Dr Alim Bey Caddesi** – is the prefect way to spend a few Turkish Lira and exercise the credit cards. Around the main yacht basin there are some excellent modern boutiques with prices on a par with those at home.

There is a craft market on Tuesdays in Bodrum, and Friday is the day for the produce market.

home to the **Museum of Underwater Archaeology** (see page 43) displaying unique collections of ancient artefacts. There are superb views across Bodrum and the sea from the extensive walls and parapets, and you can enjoy a glass of wine in the bar in the English Tower.
ⓐ On the harbour front ⓣ 0252 316 2516 ⓛ 08.30–12.00 & 13.00–17.30 Tues–Sun; closed Mon; some parts of the museum open at different hours (see page 43) ⓘ Admission charge

Day gület trip

There is a huge choice of boats offering day trips from the harbour. You will sail around several islands in the Gulf of Gökova, one of the prime sailing landscapes in the Mediterranean, and stop for swimming at lunchtime. Camel Bay is a popular stop. Most trips follow the same itinerary: out to Kara Ada Island with its hot springs, then on to Ada Boğazi for snorkelling. The final stop is at Kargı, with its camel rides.

Dedeman Aqua Park

This has a range of rides and pools.
ⓐ Kavakali Sarnia Caddesi Sokak 1 (on the road to Ortakent) at the

Dedeman Hotel ⓣ 0252 313 8500 ⓛ 10.00–18.00; closed Nov–Apr
ⓘ Admission charge

Diving

There is excellent diving all around the Bodrum coast and this is one of the best places in the eastern Mediterranean to learn to dive.

Aegean Pro Dive Center Provides PADI certification, three- and five-day packages, plus snorkelling for non-divers.
ⓐ Neyzen Tevfik Caddesi 212 ⓣ 0252 316 0737
ⓦ www.aegeanprodive.com ⓛ Apr–Oct

For information and links to other diving centres a useful website is ⓦ www.scubaturkiye.com

Mausoleum

The site of Mausolus' tomb is a bit of a disappointment. The Knights of St John recycled the stone for their castle during the early 15th century so there is little to see.

Bodrum has a wide range of handicrafts and boutiques

Turgut Reis Caddesi (above the town), signposted from the Neyzen Tevfik Caddesi 0252 316 1219 08.30–12.00 & 13.00–17.00; closed Mon Admission charge

Museum of Underwater Archaeology

Opened in 1963, several of the halls of the castle have been skilfully refurbished to display the most important collection of ancient underwater finds in Europe, discovered mainly in nearby waters. Exhibits range from the contents of ships and ship reconstructions, to arrangements of artefacts showing how they were grouped on board ship:

Ulu Burun finds The most important collection is the amazing early finds dating from the Late Bronze Age (1600–1300 BC) that show just how important sea trade was to our ancient ancestors. The world's oldest known shipwreck, the *Ulu Burun*, found in 1982, is fascinating. Excavated finds include gold jewellery from Ancient Egypt, elephant and hippopotamus ivory from central Africa, Mycenaean swords, Syrian pottery, valuable copper ingots probably picked up in Cyprus, thought to have been the copper capital of the ancient world, and many other artefacts.

East Roman Ship Set in the chapel, the East Roman Ship dates from the 7th century AD and offers a full-scale reconstruction of part of the ship and the excavation site.

The Glass Wreck Archaeologists assume that the 'glass wreck' ship was carrying a cargo of broken glass because the amount of damage to the glass items found was so extensive. Today they lie in huge piles, with some identifiable items in cases. Academics are most excited about the early Islamic glass found here. 09.00–12.00 & 14.00–16.00 Tues–Fri Extra admission charge

The Carian Princess Room or Ada Hall The exhibits here belonged to a local princess, one of the ruling family of this region during Hellenistic times (323–31 BC). The ornate tomb and selection of gold jewellery

hint at a very pampered life. 09.00–12.00 & 14.00–16.00 Tues–Fri
Extra admission charge

The Blue Voyage

In the 1920s Turkish writer and native of Bodrum Cevat Şakir Kabaağaçlı wrote *Mavi Yolculuk* (*Blue Voyage*) about a simple *gület* (traditional wooden boat) journey from Bodrum around the Lycian coast to the south, capturing the imagination of a generation of Turks. The journey described in *Blue Voyage* takes several days, but follow in Kabaağaçlı's path by taking a day trip from the harbour. One of the best charter agencies in the area is **Aegean Yachting** 0252 316 1517 0252 316 5749 www.aegeanyacht.com

TAKING A BREAK

Tarihi Yunuslar Karadeniz Pastanesi £ ❶ Traditional Turkish 'pudding' shop where you can stop for a post-dinner or pre-club sugar injection. A Bodrum institution. Dr Alim Bey Caddesi 08.00–24.00

Ali Doksan £–££ ❷ This typical *lokanta* is a down-to-earth place where you can examine the freshly cooked dishes and make your choice. It is the perfect place for a break from shopping, but get there before the local lunch crowd packs the tables at around 13.00. Indoor and outdoor dining. İnci Mah (across from the post office in the bazaar) 0232 316 6687 11.00–14.00

Sünger Pizza £ ❸ This is a long-standing and popular casual meeting place serving arguably the best pizza in town. The roof terrace offers great views over the harbour. Neyzen Tevfik Caddesi 218 0252 316 0854 11.00–24.00

Blanca ££ ❹ The entrance is deceptive until you walk in and take a table directly facing the sea. Cumhuriyet Caddesi 0252 316 8595 12.00–23.00

Epsilon £££–£££ ❺ Presided over by a Dutch flute player (who plays for guests when the mood takes her), Epsilon serves excellent Turkish/Greek-style cuisine, including some good, slow-cooked 'stew'-type dishes with the meat so tender that it falls apart. This is a place to relax in the heart of the old town. She also holds art exhibitions so you can shop and eat at the same time. ⓐ Türkkuyusu Mahallesi, Keleş Çıkmazı 5 ⓣ 0252 313 2964 ⓛ 19.00–24.00; closed Nov–Apr

Antique Theatre Hotel £££ ❻ This is easily the best restaurant in town. The owners of the excellent small hotel have lived in Paris for many years and have brought haute cuisine to the Aegean. The tables spill out from a small dining room around the pool and the menu uses the finest ingredients (it includes champagne sauces). Antique Theatre has received excellent press reviews around the world. It is certainly a great place to book if you feel inclined to splash out. ⓐ Kıbrıs Şehitleri Caddesi 243 (across from the antique theatre) ⓣ 0252 316 6053 ⓦ www.antiquetheatrehotel.com ⓛ 19.00–22.00

▲ *Enjoy a coffee by the marina*

Denizhan £££ ❼ Opened in 1988, this is a great upmarket Turkish kitchen that has not lost sight of its roots. Known locally as '*Et-Lokantası*' (meat restaurant), it is a meat-lover's delight where even the humble kepab is turned into an event with metre-long skewers brought to your table. The management recently opened the Denizhan Bistrot in downtown Bodrum (Neyzen Tevfik Caddesi), with a light menu of sandwiches, grills, pastas and *carpaccios*. ⓐ Turgut Reis Yolu (about 2.5 km/1½ miles west of town across from the Tofaş/Fiat Garage) ⓣ 0252 363 7674 ⓦ www.denizhan.com ⓛ 12.00–24.00

Kocadon £££ ❽ Traditional Turkish and Mediterranean dishes are served in this more formal establishment. The garden, with its old olive press, makes a wonderful place to eat in the centre of town. Seafood combines with traditional Ottoman dishes. ⓐ Saray Sokak 1, near the mosque in the inner harbour ⓣ 0252 316 3705 ⓛ 19.00–00.30; closed Nov–Apr ⓘ Reservations recommended

AFTER DARK

Bar Street One long alleyway runs for about 2 km (1 mile) one block in from the water's edge. It is officially known by two names, Dr Alim Bey Caddesi (Street) and Cumhuriyet Caddesi, but is known to everyone in Bodrum as 'Bar Street', where the music and the waiters vie for your money. Head for whatever sound you like, from top-40 pop to techno, but here are a few venues you may want to try.

Fora ❾ The night scene gets going around midnight and pulses away until dawn. ⓐ Bar Street ⓣ 0252 316 2244 ⓦ www.forabar.com

Hadigari ❿ Turkish for 'let's go', Hadigari is a combined restaurant, bar and nightclub. Jazz music accompanies dinner, but later the music changes to dance and trance. It has a hipper clientele than some of the bars along 'Bar Street'. ⓐ Bar Street ⓣ 0252 313 1960 ⓛ 18.00–04.00; dinner 18.00–24.00

Halikarnas ⓫ The Bodrum legend, Halikarnas, is one of the most famous clubs in the world. With a capacity of 5,000, it is a huge place and employs all the toys and ploys to make your night as memorable as possible, including the odd celebrity client. If you come to Bodrum, you really cannot go home without coming here. ⓐ Cumhuriyet Caddesi 178 ⓣ 0252 316 8000 ⓦ www.halikarnas.com.tr ◷ 22.00–05.00

Küba Bar ⓬ A favourite among wealthy Turks, this courtyard bar/restaurant plays jazz and Latin music and has a much more low-key atmosphere than some of the other bars in the street. The restaurant is expensive. ⓐ Neyzen Tevfik Caddesi 62 ⓣ 0252 313 4450 ◷ 21.00–04.00

Marine Club Catamaran ⓭ One of the most unusual nightclubs in Turkey, Marine Club Catamaran is set on a catamaran that heads out to sea every night so you can 'boogie' offshore. There is a glass dance floor so you can enjoy the sea life while you cavort to music played by guest DJs. The boat returns to shore at 05.00, but you can leave early by getting the club taxi back to shore. ⓐ Dr Alim Bey Caddesi ⓣ 0252 313 3600 ⓦ www.clubbodrum.com ◷ 01.00–05.00

M&M ⓮ Another excellent club that is a favourite – you will need to dress up to get in here. Great music with regular guest DJs from around Europe. ⓐ Dr Alim Bey Caddesi 4 ⓣ 0252 316 2725 ◷ 22.00–05.00

Mavi ⓯ Bodrum's oldest café still attracts Turkish intellectuals through the day who come here to read their papers while enjoying a morning coffee or afternoon *rakı*. As the sun sets it is a great place to enjoy live Turkish music and has a much more authentic feel than some of the disco bars along the street. ⓐ Cumhuriyet Caddesi 175 ⓣ 0252 316 3932 ◷ 07.00–02.00

Mumlu ⓰ This converted Ottoman mansion offers a great Turkish night out with dinner and performances. ⓐ Taşlik Sokak, Taşlik Cikmazi ⓣ 0252 313 8462 ⓛ 20.30–00.30. Performances from 21.00 hours

Red Lion ⓱ There is always a lively atmosphere here – one of the longest-established club/bars in town. You can come dressed to impress, and will be able to get your favourite cocktails and enjoy great music every night. ⓐ Cumhuriyet Caddesi 137 ⓣ 0252 316 3748 ⓦ www.redlion.com.tr/bar ⓛ 11.00–03.00

Sensi Bar ⓲ Sensi has a little bit of everything and is a popular choice with holidaying Brits. English and Scottish football games, karaoke and almost evening-long 'happy hours' are the major draws. ⓐ Bar Street ⓣ 0252 316 6845 ⓦ www.sensibar.com ⓛ 11.00–04.00

Gümbet

Gümbet has really come of age over the last decade. It started life as a satellite of nearby Bodrum, providing hotel accommodation for the more established resort. Today it is a fully fledged destination in its own right, with a loyal band of mainly young fans.

Gümbet (pronounced Guumbet) does not have any highbrow intentions. There are no ancient sites or museums to put on your itinerary. What it does provide is everything you need for a fun-filled foreign holiday.

The beach has lots of fine sand, and a gentle gradient with shallow water makes it perfect for sun worshippers, families and watersports enthusiasts. The streets are crammed with restaurants and bars serving English, Chinese, Mexican and even Japanese food – plus Turkish, of course – and in the evenings when the strings of rope lights come on at dusk, the resort starts buzzing with music from the hundreds of bars whose tables line the streets. You can party till dawn here – it is not a place that will suit those who are looking for peace and quiet.

Gümbet means 'water cistern', a reference to the white, round-domed water-collection buildings that dot the Bodrum peninsula.

THINGS TO SEE & DO

Because Gümbet is only a couple of kilometres (about a mile) from Bodrum, you will be able to enjoy all 'Things to see & do' (pages 40–44) of Bodrum as well as the following:

Boat trips

There is a huge choice of boat trips. You will sail around several islands in the Gulf of Gökova with a stop for swimming and, of course, for lunch. **Camel Bay** is a popular stop. Here you can enjoy a ride on one of these rather unpredictable 'ships of the desert'. Most trips follow the same itinerary, heading out to **Kara Ada Island** with its hot springs, then

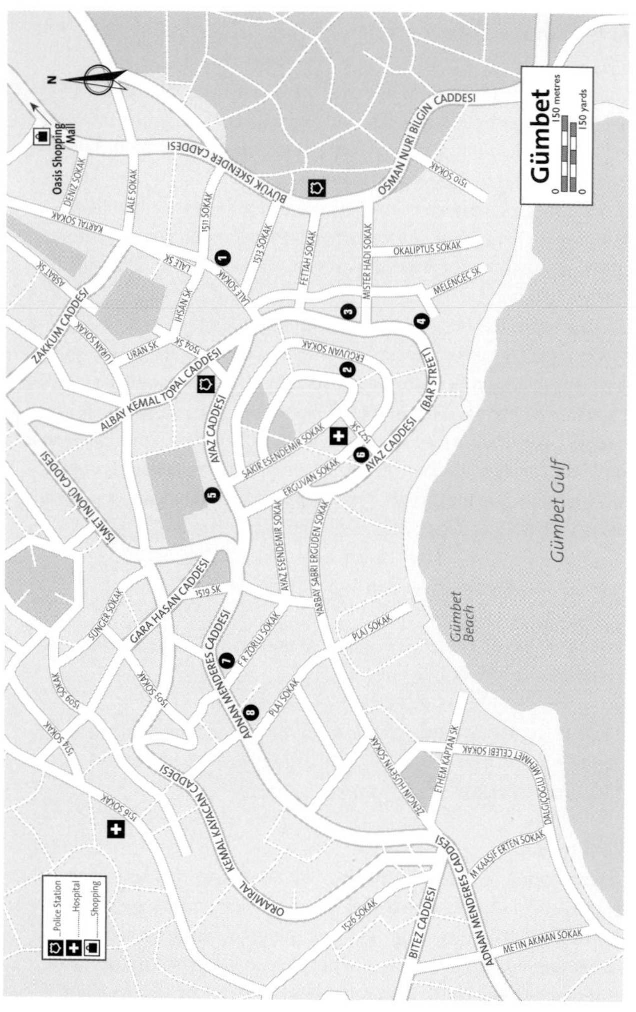
Gümbet
0 150 metres
0 150 yards
N
Oasis Shopping Mall
BÜYÜK ISKENDER CADDESI
OSMAN NURI BILGIN CADDESI
1510 SOKAK
DENIZ SOKAK
LALE SOKAK
KARTAL SOKAK
1511 SOKAK
1513 SOKAK
FETTAH SOKAK
MISTER HADI SOKAK
OKALIPTUS SOKAK
MELENGEC SK
ASBAT SK
LALE SK
LALE SOKAK
IHSAN SK
ZAKKUM CADDESI
URAN SOKAK
URAN SK
1504 SK
ERGUVAN SOKAK
ALBAY KEMAL TOPAL CADDESI
AYAZ CADDESI
(BAR STREET)
1521 SK
SAKIR ESENDEMIR SOKAK
ERGUVAN SOKAK
ISMET INÖNÜ CADDESI
AYAZ ESENDEMIR SOKAK
YARBAY SABRI ERGÜDEN SOKAK
1519 SK
GARA HASAN CADDESI
SÜNGER SOKAK
ADNAN MENDERES CADDESI
F.R ZORLU SOKAK
PLAJ SOKAK
1509 SOKAK
1503 SOKAK
1514 SOKAK
KEMAL KAYACAN CADDESI
1516 SOKAK
ZENCIN HÜSEYIN SOKAK
ETHEM KAPTAN SK
MEHMET CELEBI SOKAK
DALGIÇOĞLU MEHMET
M.KAASIF ERTEN SOKAK
ORAMIRAL
1526 SOKAK
BITEZ CADDESI
ADNAN MENDERES CADDESI
METIN AKMAN SOKAK
Gümbet Beach
Gümbet Gulf
Police Station
Hospital
Shopping
1
2
3
4
5
6
7
8

SHOPPING

Aside from the normal souvenir shops, Gümbet has the Bodrum peninsula's first shopping centre – **Oasis** – with well-known names such as Quiksilver, Cacharel and Marks & Spencer. ⓐ Kibris Şehitleri Caddesi ⓣ 0252 317 0002 ⓦ www.oasisbodrum.com

moving on to **Ada Boğazı** for snorkelling. The final stop is at **Kargı**, which also has camel rides.

Cinema

The Oasis Shopping Centre (see box, above) has a five-screen complex featuring Hollywood blockbusters in English with Turkish subtitles.

Watersports

Kiosks on the beach offer a full range of activities, from jet-skiing and parasailing to banana-boat rides. You can rent by the hour or by the session.

TAKING A BREAK

Windy Bay Beach Steak and Wine House £ ❶ A cheap and cheerful place for a quick lunch. It is on Bar Street, which means it is a great pit-stop when you get the munchies during the evening. Concentrates on burgers, pizzas and omelettes – plus an English Sunday lunch. ⓐ Ayaz Caddesi (Bar Street) ⓛ 08.00–01.00

AFTER DARK

Angus Steak House ££ ❷ The views across Gümbet Bay from the terrace are a lovely accompaniment to your meal. The restaurant serves a range of Turkish dishes, but it is the steaks (not surprising given the name) that have gained a reputation since they opened in 1993. ⓐ Şakir Esendemir Sokak 4 ⓣ 0252 313 3992 ⓛ 18.00–01.00

Chinese Lotus ££ ❸ The name is a little misleading because Mexican, Indian and Turkish food is on the menu as well as steaks. ⓐ Ayaz Caddesi (Bar Street) ⓣ 0252 319 5468 ⓛ 11.00–01.00

The Green Dragon ££ ❹ Opened in 1990, this was the first Chinese restaurant in the resort. It has branched out into other types of food and you can now enjoy Indian, Mexican, Italian and Turkish here – there should be something for everyone. ⓐ Gümbet Mevkii, Ayaz Caddesi (Bar Street) 20 ⓣ 0252 316 1504 ⓛ 11.00–24.00

Mystery Bar ❺ The Mystery Bar is one of the late-evening haunts; below is the karaoke bar, which is always good for a laugh. Either dance or sit on bar stools in this stylish disco with futuristic metallic decor, including blue walls and silver tables. ⓐ Ayaz Caddesi (Bar Street) ⓣ 0252 313 1868 ⓛ 11.00–04.00

Outback Bar ❻ This famous Aussie surf bar has become an institution with its great beach location, signature fishbowl cocktails, good old rock music, pool and relaxed attitudes. Outback Bar 2 is now open, so you have two places from which to watch the sunset and sunrise. ⓐ Just off Bar Street ⓦ www.theoutbackbar.com ⓛ 24 hours

Talk of the Town ❼ Three UK drag artists star in the nightly *Dream Girls Show*. They dress lavishly and pepper their acts with plenty of saucy British humour. ⓐ Adnan Menderes Caddesi 20 ⓣ 0252 313 4621 ⓛ 19.30–02.00 ⓘ Admission charge includes dinner and a drink

Yucca ❽ One of the trendiest spots in Gümbet, catering for almost all types of food. Live entertainment is available after 22.00 daily and the place is always busy, so be sure to go early. ⓐ Adnan Menderes Caddesi 55 ⓛ 11.00–01.00

Relax with a drink by the beach in Gümbet

The Bodrum peninsula

The verdant rocky coastline of the Bodrum peninsula is one of the world's top yachting destinations, with numerous attractive anchorages where a private dinner can be enjoyed plus excellent swimming and snorkelling. The countryside is made up of a series of dramatic forested ridges now dotted with *gümbets* (traditional water cisterns), stone towers, ruined churches and windmills.

Scattered around are a handful of small and exclusive resorts where you can take it easy and simply enjoy that novel you always meant to read, or snorkel in the pristine waters. These resorts are really all about quiet relaxation – although you will find excellent restaurants, nightlife is limited to an after-dinner stroll along the beach or a cocktail under the stars. However, all these resorts offer easy bus or taxi access to Bodrum and Gümbet for days of sightseeing and nights of action for those who want it.

The large marina at Turgut Reis

Bitez

Bitez is the biggest of these peninsula resorts, and the second most popular resort in Turkey for windsurfers after Çeşme (see page 15). It is also an important marina, although the beach is small.
ⓐ 10 km (6 miles) from Bodrum

Dedeman Resort This has the Life Style Health and Beauty Centre, covering an area of 2,250 sq m (2,462 sq yds), with sauna, massage, solarium, Turkish bath and Jacuzzi plus fitness classes. There is also a 'Freshtaurant' with healthy food and drinks.
ⓐ Gündönümü Mevkii, Bitez ⓣ 0252 313 8500
ⓦ www.dedemanhotels.com

Spafuga This small but well-equipped spa in a 'boutique' hotel offers shiatsu, aromatherapy and other massage treatments.
ⓐ Fuga Hotel, Asarlık Mevkii ⓣ 0252 317 2360 ⓦ www.fuga.com.tr

Göltürkbükü

This upmarket little enclave (pronounced Gerl-tuurk-buu-kuu), made up of Türkbükü and its neighbouring village Gölköy, is the summer home of many arty types from Istanbul. Those who do not have houses here arrive on their yachts. There is no beach here and swimming is from a concrete lido.
ⓐ On the northern coast of the peninsula, north of Bodrum

Gümüşlük

The prettiest of the peninsula's settlements, Gümüşlük is subject to a preservation order and its centre is traffic free. The name is taken from a form of silver, which used to be mined close by, although locals say that it is because the sea is phosphorescent and glows in the dark at certain times of the year. The modern sleepy village occupies the site of ancient Myndos and you can wander among what is left of the ruins.
ⓐ 23 km (14 miles) from Bodrum

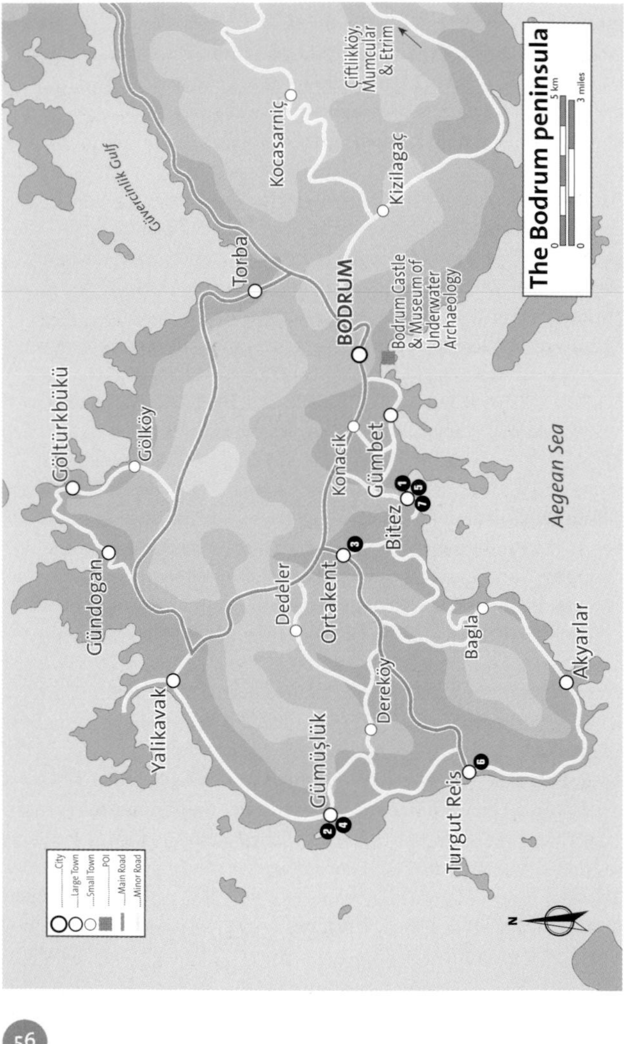

The Bodrum peninsula

0 5 km
0 3 miles

City
Large Town
Small Town
POI
Main Road
Minor Road

N

Göltürkbükü
Gündogan
Gölköy
Güvercinlik Gulf
Yalikavak
Torba
Kocasarniç
Dedeler
Gümüşlük
Ortakent
Konacik
BODRUM
Çiftlikköy, Mumcular & Etrim
Dereköy
Gümbet
Bitez
Kizilagaç
Bodrum Castle & Museum of Underwater Archaeology
Turgut Reis
Bagla
Akyarlar
Aegean Sea

Ortakent

This inland village offers access to a number of beaches, including the 2 km (1 mile) long Yahşi Yalı and Kargi or Camel Beach – reached also on many day boat trips from Bodrum – where you can take a camel ride. The town has one of the finest examples of the traditional stone towers, the 17th-century Mustafa Paşa Tower.

12 km (7 miles) from Bodrum

Torba

The modern resort of Torba makes a great base for watersports and sailing, but there are also ancient remains to explore – a round stone structure said to be 2,500 years old plus a Byzantine monastery left to the elements long ago.

8 km (5 miles) north of Bodrum

Turgut Reis

Turgut Reis is named after a famous Turkish naval commander, Derya Turgut Reis, who lived there in the 16th century. Today Turgut Reis is a magnet for sailors, with a large marina, but it also has some amazing renovated Ottoman mansions clinging to the forested hillsides rising from the waterline.

On the southwest tip of the peninsula, 5 km (3 miles) from the Greek Island of Kos (see page 92)

TAKING A BREAK

Mado £ ❶ Part of a chain of Turkish 'patisseries', Mado serves excellent ice cream plus snacks such as *börek* and toasted sandwiches. Perfect for a light lunch. Şah Caddesi, Bitez Yolu Mevkii 16, Bitez 0252 363 9231 09.00–01.00

Gümüşcafé £–££ ❷ With its pretty waterside setting, this small café makes a good place for a relaxed meal. The menu is quite extensive, with some excellent Turkish casseroles as well as French and Italian dishes.

Vegetarians and vegans are also catered for. Snacks are served throughout the day. ⓐ Yalı Mevkii, Gümüşlük ⓣ 0252 349 4234 ⓛ 08.00–02.00

AFTER DARK

Sakız Ana £ ❸ An excellent family kitchen restaurant where you can try authentic, fresh, home-cooked Turkish cuisine. No frills, just tasty food, at lunchtimes only. ⓐ Yahşi 133, Ortakent ⓣ 0252 348 3703 ⓛ 12.00–17.00

Ali Rıza'nın Yeri ££ ❹ On the waterfront at Gümüşlük, this fish restaurant is one of the best, with a long-standing local clientele. It is not very expensive for fish (although of course fish is always the most expensive dish), and the quality is good. ⓐ Yalı Mevkii, Gümüşlük ⓣ 0252 394 3047

Ambrosia ££ ❺ Above-average buffet food and the most entertaining live shows on the peninsula. ⓐ Bitez Beach ⓣ 0252 343 1886 ⓛ 19.30–22.00

Mehtap Restaurant ££ ❻ Open for more than 20 years, this fish restaurant was one of the first in the resort. It overlooks a small marina and offers a good selection of fresh fish and grilled meats. ⓐ Akyarlar, Turgut Reis ⓣ 0252 393 6148 ⓛ 12.00–24.00

Vona £££ ❼ Dine under palm trees and enjoy a steak with Gorgonzola cheese sauce or skewered sole; vegetarian choices also. ⓐ Bitez Beach ⓣ 0252 363 7618 ⓛ 19.00–23.00

Turkey offers many opportunities for relaxing in a spa

EXCURSIONS
Out & about

Around the Aegean

THINGS TO SEE & DO

Gület cruise

It is really not a true Turkish holiday if you do not get out onto the water. From offshore you can really appreciate the beauty of the landscape, the verdant pine forests, olive groves and unspoilt beaches and coves. You may even be lucky enough to spot a dolphin or a turtle.

The *gület*, a traditional Turkish wooden boat, is one of the most beautiful and distinctive crafts in the Mediterranean and you will find them in all Turkish ports. You can rent them privately, but there is a choice of day trips for a very reasonable price. You can enjoy lunch and take a swim before returning to your resort at about 17.00 or 18.00 in time to shower and change for your evening meal.

Jeep or 4x4 safari

The jeep safari is a real adventure. Out and about on roads you would probably never find yourself in a rental car, it gives you a chance to see the traditional Turkish way of life and discover the countryside around your resort. The day includes a traditional lunch and a spot of shopping at a craft market or carpet warehouse. Routes vary with each company, but the following are some of the places you might head out to from the main resorts:

From Bodrum Explore the interior of the Bodrum peninsula and its numerous small villages – including Çiftlikköy, Etrim or Mumcular – plus some breathtaking forest and mountain scenery. You stop at a remote cove for a swim before returning to your hotel.

From Çeşme The rocky and sparsely populated Çeşme peninsula is the perfect place to get 'off the beaten track'. Head out to marvel at the old and often abandoned Greek villages, not populated since the 1920s.

From Kuşadası You can drive south to the Dilek National Park on the Davutlar peninsula, one of the last refuges of the rare Anatolian

wild cat. After visiting the fortifications and driving through some spectacular forest scenery you can take a dip in the fresh spring water in the Zeus cave.

Shop in the markets

Inland towns hold large regional markets, usually once a week, and they are a great place to shop somewhere different from the tourist bazaars in the main resorts. Turks travel from small villages all around the area to shop for food and livestock and to socialise. It is a great place to watch them bargaining over prices or enjoying a tea in the cafés.

A sizeable town inland from Bodrum and its satellite resorts, Milas holds one of the largest and most authentic markets in the area. Fake designer labels sit side by side with a huge range of Turkish handicrafts, but the market is particularly known for its good selection of carpets. The traditional colours of Milas carpets are more muted than those of carpets produced in other areas, but there is a good choice from around Turkey. Because it is not just a tourist market, prices are generally less expensive than those in the resorts.

From Kuşadası and Altınkum, Söke is the place to be – the Wednesday market is not quite as large as the one at Milas, but the range of goods on offer is good and again you can enjoy the authentic atmosphere.

Hamams (Turkish baths)

Not only will you be squeaky clean and relaxed, but your suntan will last far longer. So what better reason to try a traditional Turkish bath, or, as the Turks call it, a *hamam*.

History Cleanliness is very important in Islamic cultures, where face, hands and feet must be clean before each prayer session. The communal *hamams* were a place where hot water could be guaranteed and where men or women could come and have a good gossip. During Ottoman times it was grounds for divorce if a man refused his wife bath money. Today, although many town houses and apartments have all the mod cons, it is still a popular social activity.

What to expect Traditional *hamams* have separate sessions for men and women, but the owners of *hamams* in tourist areas understand that visitors have different attitudes and will run mixed sessions.

When you enter a *hamam* you are given a *peştamal* (gown) and wooden sandals to wear. You can go naked under the robe or wear a swimming costume, bikini or shorts.

Then you go into the *hararet*, or steam room, where you are hit by a wall of hot air. Go to one of the basins and wash yourself all over. When you wash the suds off, do not get any back in the basin because this needs to be kept clean for other customers. You then lie on the *göbek taşı*, or navel stone, the marble slab at the centre of the room. Relax for 15 minutes or so to let the heat open up the pores. Your masseur or *tellak* will then rub you with a rough cloth covered in soap to slough off any grime and dead skin cells. Then you are pummelled and rubbed until you

Try your luck at bartering for souvenir goods

feel as though your arms and legs might fall off. After another shower, you leave the hot room, wrap yourself in a thick robe and relax with a cup of tea. Do not rush this part because you need to cool down and let your body adjust to the treatment.

A Turkish evening

Genuine Turkish food and entertainment may be difficult to find in many modern resorts, but the 'Turkish evening' offers the perfect introduction to the culture and it is a really fun evening out. You will start with a buffet meal of *meze* dishes, barbecued meats and salads washed down with local wine or beer (see page 95 for more details of traditional foods), after which you will be entertained by folk dances, plus of course the famous 'belly dance'. Someone from the audience is always invited to have a go, which is generally amusing for everyone watching. Later in the evening the dance floor is handed over to the guests for an hour or so of disco dancing.

Village tours

Most Aegean resorts have lost their traditional ways of life, so a village tour is the perfect way to see how the vast majority of Turks live. Visit a rural Turkish home where the women cook and make tea, enter a local mosque or watch carpet weaving and other traditional crafts.

From Bodrum Take a trip through fragrant pine forest to the farming village of Çamlık.

From Çeşme Go to the peninsula villages, where decaying Greek mansions and windmills are set among the orange groves.

From Kuşadası Visit Şirince, an old Greek hill town which is known for its traditional 19th-century village houses, handicrafts and rural way of life. Wine is produced in this small hillside Turkish village.

Foça

The perfect place for an afternoon of relaxed sightseeing, Foça is a fishing village turned resort that has not yet lost its charm. It is a favourite spot for weekenders from nearby İzmir, so you will be among Turks relaxing and enjoying themselves. They come to stroll in the old town, sit in the cafés and eat at the excellent authentic restaurants along the seafront.

HISTORY

Founded by Ionian peoples in around 1000 BC, the town was originally Phocaea. The city became known for its shipbuilding and seafaring skills. Its huge ships, powered by 50 or more oarsmen, sailed all around the Mediterranean. It is even said that the Phocaeans landed in southern France and founded a settlement that is now the city of Marseilles. Later, Phocaea became a Byzantine trading port before being given as a gift to the Genoese who protected the trade routes to western Europe. It finally fell into the hands of the Ottomans and settled down as a simple fishing village.

THINGS TO SEE & DO

For more information on things to see and do in Foça, contact the tourist office ⓐ Şahil Caddesi, in the main square ⓣ 0232 812 1222

Ancient theatre

This small theatre dates from *c.* 340 BC.
ⓐ On the eastern outskirts of town

Beşkapılar (the Castle)

This part Byzantine/part Genoese structure dominates the waterfront and is the most impressive building in town, although it has been rather crudely renovated and had a couple of towers added.
ⓛ Closed to the public

Boat trips

In ancient Greek, *phocaea* means 'seal' and the town took its name from the noisy monk seals that populated the bay's rocky shores and islets. Today, the few that are left are protected by the Turkish government, but you can take a trip from the harbour to watch them lazing on the rocks.

Fatih Camii

Built in the 15th century after the Ottoman takeover, this small mosque has some delicate interior decoration.

ⓐ Eski Adliye Sokak

Old town

A tiny maze of alleyways makes up the old town and you can wander among whitewashed cottages and Ottoman mansions that now house boutiques and café/bars.

Old town of Foça

Pergamum

One of the most dramatic ancient sites in Turkey, Pergamum was capital of the region of Asia Minor in the 3rd century BC before Ephesus took over (see page 75). The city was also home to an important medical school, and people travelled to it from far and wide for treatment.

Historical records tell us that Pergamum had beautiful and ornate buildings, but when the first archaeologists arrived from Germany in the 19th century, they took the best bits home with them and many of them are now on display at the Pergamon Museum in Berlin. However, the city is not a disappointment – the stunning location and marvellous theatre make it worth a visit, as is the nearby modern town of Bergama, famed for its carpets.

HISTORY

Founded in 301 BC, the city was Rome's first friendly ally in the area, but although it grew rich and powerful very quickly, by the 2nd century AD it had lost its influence. The two main archaeological sites, the Acropolis (upper city) and the Asclepion (ancient centre of healing), lie a few kilometres apart. Much of ancient Pergamum probably lies undiscovered underneath the family homes you see today.

THINGS TO SEE & DO

Acropolis

Located 280 m (919 ft) above Bergama and the surrounding countryside, the Acropolis has a spectacular setting, with panoramic views out towards the Aegean. The theatre, with as many as 78 rows of seats, cascades down the steep natural drop of the hill. On the hilltop plateau sit the partly re-erected remains of the 2nd-century AD Temple of Trajan.
ⓐ Kale Yolu, signposted 5 km (3 miles) above Bergama ⓑ 08.00–19.00 May–Oct; 08.00–17.00 Nov–Apr ⓘ Admission charge

Archaeological Museum

Although many of Pergamum's finest treasures are now overseas, there are still a few at the site. The figure of Nike (Winged Victory) displayed here has become an emblem of the city and there are elements of ornate friezes and pediments that hint at the splendour now missing. One of the most impressive pieces, a statue of Aphrodite, was found at another site nearby. The museum also has a small selection of later traditional costumes and handicrafts in its ethnography section.

Bankalar Caddesi 08.30–17.30 Tues–Sun Admission charge

Asclepion

This ancient health complex was state of the art during the Roman era, 2,000 years ago. You can walk along the western section of Via Tecta, a marble colonnaded road that connected the Acropolis to the sanctuary, and explore the remains of a temple complex and diagnosis room.

Asclepion Caddesi, 1 km (½ mile) south of Bergama, off the main road 08.00–19.00 May–Oct; 08.00–17.00 Nov–Apr Admission charge

Red Basilica

Originally built as a temple to the Egyptian gods Harpokrates, Isis and Serapis in the 2nd century AD, this huge red stone building was converted into a Christian basilica in the 4th century (one of the original Seven Churches of Asia Minor) and now has a mosque within the walls.

Intersection of Kasapoğlu Caddesi and Bankalar Caddesi

08.30–17.30 Admission charge

EXCURSION

Bergama

The centre of Bergama has some excellent timber-framed Ottoman mansions in its old quarter, where you can stroll amongst some of the Aegean's best carpet shops, selling traditional Bergama styles (characterised by their deep red colour), and some good antiques shops. Prices can be high here, but so is quality.

A few kilometres outside Pergamum

Sardis

Once an important ancient city, much of Sardis is hidden under the village of Sart and the farmland around it. There is not a lot to see – it is nowhere near the size of Pergamum or Ephesus – but each building or sector excavated is either of exceptional quality or beauty, or offers the visitor something unusual or interesting.

HISTORY

The discovery of gold in the River Pactolus close by guaranteed that Sardis would be a successful city. Founded 5,000 years ago, it was capital of the Lydian Kingdom (*c.* 685 BC) and one of its rulers, King Croesus (*c.* 561–548 BC), was said to be the richest man in the world, giving rise to the saying 'rich as Croesus'. The Lydians were conquered by Alexander the Great but the city continued to thrive under Greek and Roman rule.

THINGS TO SEE & DO

For more information on things to see and do in Sardis, contact the tourist office ⓐ Sahil Caddesi, in the main square ⓣ 0232 812 1222

Ruins of the synagogue at Sardis

MYTHS OF THE RIVER PACTOLUS

The Midas Touch

According to Greek myth, King Midas was responsible for putting the gold in the River Pactolus. The gods granted him his wish that everything he touched should turn to gold, but when this became a curse – he could not eat or drink anything – he pleaded with the gods to take the power back. When he washed his hands in the river, the gold in his body was released into the water and Midas was mortal again.

The Golden Fleece

It is possible that there is a practical basis to the mythological story of the 'golden fleece'. In ancient times the Greeks would 'pan' for gold by putting sheepskins in the River Pactolus. Tiny pieces of metal on the river bottom would get caught in the fine wool. When the skin was taken out of the water and dried the gold would fall out and could be collected and smelted.

Imperial Hall

This 3rd-century AD two-storey brick and marble building was the town's bath and sports complex, but the front facade is one of the finest in Turkey, decorated with fluted columns, marble friezes and an intricately carved pediment crowning the two sets of entrance arches. Unfortunately, the 1¼ ha (3 acre) complex behind it is still mostly piles of stone and brick. The best time to view the façade is in the mornings, when the sun shines directly on it.

Marble Way

This is an excellent section of ancient roadway that has been carefully excavated in the heart of Sardis. The Byzantine boulevard is 18 m (20 yds) wide, with a thick marble base now worn by the cart tracks that passed along here for centuries. The road was lined with shops, but now only the foundations of the walls and a few sections of mosaic can be seen.

Synagogue

The 3rd-century synagogue has some impressive decoration, particularly its mosaics. Those on the floor are original, but the wall decoration is reconstructed. The originals are in the museum in nearby Manisa.
Ⓐ Main road in Sart 🕒 08.30–20.00 summer; 08.30–17.30 winter
❗ Admission charge

Temple of Artemis

When archaeologists first arrived at the temple site in 1910, only the tops of two columns stuck out of the soil. Built *c.* 200 BC, the site had been abandoned after an earthquake in AD 17. Measuring 99 m by 45 m (108 by 49 yds), the temple was one of the largest religious sites in the Greek world, even larger than the Parthenon in Athens. The temple platform and a handful of Ionic columns convey an impression of the size and beauty of the finished temple.
Ⓐ 1 km (½ mile) south of Sart, signposted from the village
🕒 08.30–20.00 summer; 08.30–17.30 winter ❗ Admission charge

Ruins of the Temple of Artemis

İzmir

The third-largest city in Turkey and its largest port, İzmir does not make a good first impression. It is huge, hot and dusty, with hillsides festooned with concrete apartment blocks. But İzmir was once the ancient Greek city of Smyrna, and for many centuries the eastern terminus of the silk route from China, so it has a great history, plus one of the most authentic bazaars in western Turkey.

HISTORY

Until World War I, the population of İzmir was mostly of Greek descent. These people had lived there since ancient times and stayed after the Ottomans took Turkey in the 15th century. İzmir saw some of the fiercest fighting during Turkey's War of Independence in the early 1920s, and much of the historic town was destroyed. Finally, the Greek population left en masse.

THINGS TO SEE & DO

For more information on things to see and do in İzmir, contact the tourist office ⓐ Gazi Osman Paşa Bul in the Büyük Efes Hotel ⓣ 0232 484 4300

Alsancak District

Although large sections of the city burned to the ground in the violence of the 1920s, this small quarter escaped and displays some lovely 18th- and 19th-century Greek-style mansions. In the last 20 years, plenty of money has been poured into renovating the district, but you will also find characterful houses that are still in need of care and attention.

Archaeological Museum

This is one of the most comprehensive collections in Turkey, with pieces from all the major archaeological sites in the northern Aegean and all eras of the country's long history.

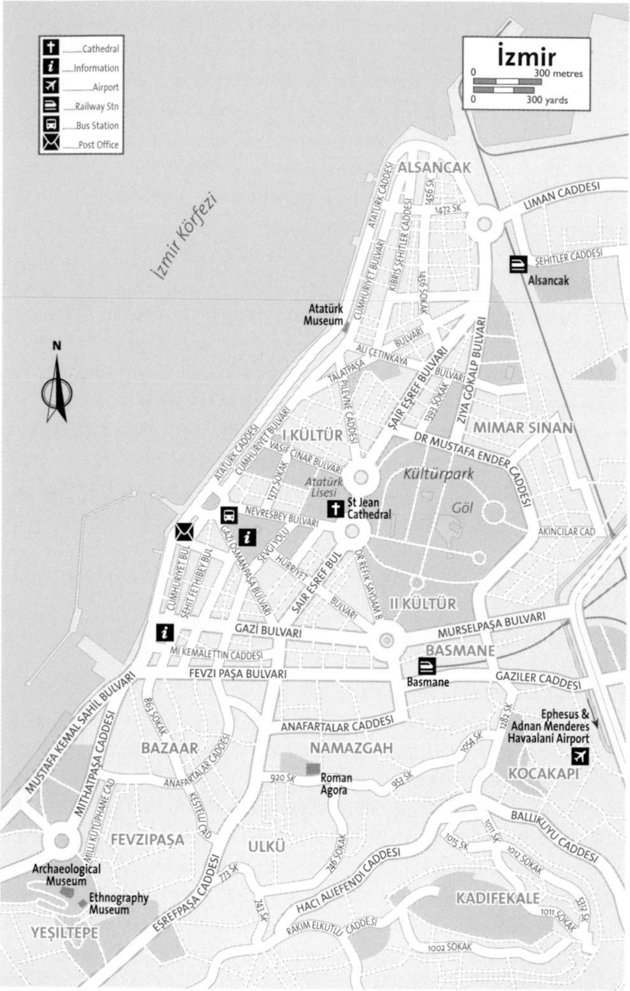

İzmir

0 300 metres
0 300 yards

Cathedral
Information
Airport
Railway Stn
Bus Station
Post Office

N

İzmir Körfezi
ALSANCAK
ATATÜRK CADDESİ
1456 SK
1472 SK
KIBRIS ŞEHİTLER CADDESİ
CUMHURİYET BULVARI
1456 SOKAK
LIMAN CADDESİ
ŞEHİTLER CADDESİ
Alsancak
Atatürk Museum
ALİ ÇETİNKAYA BULVARI
TALATPAŞA BULVARI
PILEVNE CADDESİ
ŞAIR EŞREF BULVARI
1393 SOKAK
ZIYA GÖKALP BULVARI
MIMAR SINAN
I KÜLTÜR
DR MUSTAFA ENDER CADDESİ
VASIF ÇINAR BULVARI
Kültürpark
Atatürk Lisesi
1377 SOKAK
St Jean Cathedral
Göl
NEVRESBEY BULVARI
GAZİ OSMANPAŞA BULVARI
SEVGİ YOLU
HÜRRİYET BULVARI
AKINCILAR CAD
CUMHURİYET BUL
ŞEHİT FETHİBEY BUL
ŞAIR EŞREF BUL
DR REFIK SAYDAM B
II KÜLTÜR
GAZİ BULVARI
MURSELPAŞA BULVARI
MI KEMALETTIN CADDESİ
BASMANE
FEVZI PAŞA BULVARI
Basmane
GAZILER CADDESİ
MUSTAFA KEMAL SAHİL BULVARI
863 SOKAK
MITHATPAŞA CADDESİ
ANAFARTALAR CADDESİ
1282 SK
Ephesus & Adnan Menderes Havaalani Airport
BAZAAR
NAMAZGAH
1054 SK
KOCAKAPI
920 SK
Roman Agora
953 SK
MILLI KÜTÜPHANE CAD
KESTELLİ CAD
BALLIKUYU CADDESİ
FEVZIPAŞA
ULKÜ
1011 SK
1015 SK
1012 SOKAK
Archaeological Museum
773 SK
746 SOKAK
HACI ALİEFENDİ CADDESİ
Ethnography Museum
KADIFEKALE
743 SK
ESREFPAŞA CADDESİ
RAKIM ELKUTLU CADDESİ
1011 SOKAK
5312 SK
YEŞILTEPE
1002 SOKAK

It is in these galleries that the daily lives of the people are brought to life, with kitchen tools, decorative figurines, and intricate precious jewellery showing just how sophisticated these ancient peoples were. Larger statues and busts from the Hellenistic and Roman periods are equally impressive and have their own gallery, so you can explore how styles changed over time.

Bahri Baba Parkı 08.30–17.30 Tues–Sat, closed Mon
Admission charge

Atatürk Museum

The house itself is an interesting mixture of Greek and Ottoman styles and was owned by a Greek carpet merchant until he abandoned it in 1922. It was presented to Atatürk as a gift by the Municipality of İzmir in 1926. The president's private quarters were on the first floor and are still furnished in period style with a few of his personal belongings.

Atatürk Avenue No 24, Alsancak 08.30–17.30 Tues–Sun, closed Mon
Admission charge

Bazaar

This is not a tourist city, so more than anywhere on the Aegean coast you can find a genuine eastern shopping experience here. The bazaar is divided into different quarters selling items as mundane as buckets and washing lines to gold and carpets. It is a great place to watch the locals striking a bargain over a cup of apple tea.

West of Anafartalar Caddesi

Ethnography Museum

Turkey has very few museums that showcase Turkish Ottoman history and traditional ways of life, but this is one of the best.

The building was constructed in neoclassical style and started life as St Roch Hospital in 1831. It was opened as the museum in 1984. All aspects of 19th-century life are covered here. One of the most fascinating sections is the handicrafts exhibit, where you can see how many of the souvenirs you can buy today were made over 100 years ago.

Other exhibits include clothing, glass, traditional costumes and the reconstruction of a bridal room plus books and coins.
ⓐ Bahri Baba Parkı ⓛ 08.30–12.00 & 13.00–17.00 Tues–Sun
ⓘ Admission charge

Roman Agora

One of the biggest Roman *agoras* (marketplace and meeting area) in western Turkey, the remains here date from the 2nd century AD and include temples, shops and stoas. Excavations in the late 1990s unearthed the northern entrance gate and produced statues and smaller figurines plus lots of domestic items, including glass bottles and metal tools.
ⓐ Anafartalar Caddesi ⓛ 08.30–12.00 & 13.00–17.30
ⓘ Admission charge

Ephesus

Ephesus is the largest and most complete ancient city in the eastern Mediterranean, situated 19 km (12 miles) northeast of Kuşadası. It is a must-see site even if you are not into history. The exceptionally well-preserved buildings allow us to step back in time to life in the capital of late Roman Asia Minor.

To see the architectural detail it is best to arrive early or late in the day when the site is quiet, but the crowded streets you find when the tour groups arrive (between 10.00 and 16.00) offer the kind of genuine lively atmosphere that Ephesus would have had over 1,500 years ago.

HISTORY

Founded in the 11th century BC, Ephesus became an important and rich city because it was the centre of worship for Artemis, the goddess of fertility. The temple here was one of the Seven Wonders of the ancient world and attracted pilgrims from around ancient Greece.

Curetes Street, Ephesus

In Roman times the city was capital of Asia Minor, with a population of over 250,000 people. It was a trading and banking city of immense wealth and was one of the most advanced cities in the empire, with both flushing communal latrines and street lighting.

Ephesus was an important Christian city in the middle of the first millennium, with a close association with St Paul of Tarsus, and was populated until the 11th century AD. The last few hundred years brought serious problems when its port on the River Cayster began to silt up. Eventually it was cut off from the sea completely, making trade impossible. The city was then abandoned.

THINGS TO SEE & DO

Upper city

A plateau at the top of the hill is the least exciting part of the city. Around the wide space that was once the Upper Agora you will be able to explore the administrative headquarters of the city, a small *odeon* (theatre) and the remains of a thermal spa. The best part of the upper city is the view down over the rest of Ephesus. From the small square in front of the Monument of Memmius, which was erected in homage to the citizens of the city, you get your most breathtaking view down Curetes Street, one of the most photographed vistas in Turkey.

Beyond the buildings look out over the flat area where there is a modern airfield. This used to be the port area for the ancient city. Then search for the coast out in the distance. This is how far the sea has receded since Roman times and it shows why the city was doomed. There was no way to transport large amounts of goods efficiently over land in those days, and without a port the city could not function.

Curetes Street

The major arterial route linking the upper city with the port, Curetes Street was the Oxford Street, Briggate or Princes Street of its day. Shops selling goods from around the empire lined the thoroughfare, along with a number of important temples in between, including the Temple of

Ephesus theatre

Hadrian (built *c.* AD 117–38), with its distinctive double archway of fine Corinthian columns and elaborate frieze dedicated to the goddess Tyche.

Slope House

On each side of Curetes Street, the residential quarters of Ephesus lie on the terraced hillside, reached by narrow alleyways. These were the houses of the rich, and one three-storey residence, Yamaç Evleri, or 'Slope House', has undergone a thorough excavation to offer a glimpse of the Roman lifestyle and interior design. The spacious rooms are decorated with incredible original mosaic floors and wall frescoes that were the height of fashion.

Entry to Slope House is extra to the Ephesus ticket price, but is well worth it

Celcus Library

At the bottom of Curetes Street, the library is one of the focal points of the city. Erected in AD 117 as a memorial to Tiberius Julius Celsus by his son, it has a grandiose two-storey facade decorated with fluted columns and statues depicting the Four Virtues: Goodness (Arete), Thought (Ennoia), Knowledge (Episteme) and Wisdom (Sophia). The library once held 12,000 scrolls and was considered a great centre of learning.

Gate of Mazeus & Mithridates

Linking the Library and the neighbouring *agora*, the Gate of Mazeus and Mithridates was commissioned by two slaves freed by the Emperor Augustus who went on to become leading citizens of the city. It is built in the style of a triumphal arch.

Baths of Scolastica

The baths were one of the social centres of the city, a place where men got together to do business deals, debate politics or simply gossip. These were built in the 1st century AD in the heart of the city almost opposite the Celcus Library, and you can see the hot room and cold room.

Theatre

One of the prettiest and most complete Roman theatres, Ephesus theatre is still being used during the important Ephesus Festival of Culture and

Celcus Library

Art each May. During Roman times, 24,000 people would cram the stands to enjoy drama and comedy, and it was also the scene of many of St Paul's Evangelical speeches. He was cornered here by angry Ephesians when he criticised their beloved Artemis, but managed to escape.

Arcadian Way

One of the first Roman streets to get municipal lighting, Arcadian Way led from the theatre to the port in the 5th century AD. The widest avenue in the city, much of it is now off limits to the public, but it is possible to stand at the top (in front of the theatre) and look towards what would have been the warehouse district and waterfront during Roman times.

Marble Way

Linking Curetes Street with Arcadian Way, the short Marble Way has a couple of interesting things to see. Notice how the marble of the road surface has been worn away by the passing of hundreds of thousands of cart wheels. No doubt these carts were heavily laden with goods for market. There is also an advertisement for a brothel etched in a stone of the road, pointing the way to the entrance close by.

Temple of Artemis

A kilometre (half a mile) away from the city is the Temple of Artemis or Artemision, the most important temple to Artemis in the world. A mammoth building measuring 105 by 55 m (115 by 60 yds) and housing a life-size gold statue to the goddess, it was so impressive that it was known as one of the Seven Wonders of the ancient world; today, it is a shadow of its former self. The Goths destroyed the site in AD 262 and much of the stone was later recycled, so that only the main temple platform and a couple of lonely columns remain.

Although the gold statue of Artemis has never been found (it was probably melted down centuries ago), there are several fascinating stone and marble statues of her in the Ephesus Museum at Selçuk (see page 90).

500 m (550 yds) from Selçuk on the Kuşadası road 08.30–12.00 & 13.00–19.00 (17.00 winter) Admission charge

Pamukkale

Pamukkale (Pamuk-kalay) means 'cotton castle' in Turkish and it is a very appropriate name. Inland from the Aegean coast, and more than a day trip, this huge natural travertine (a type of crystalline rock) fountain is one of Turkey's most famous attractions and one of its most beautiful and spectacular landscapes. Here, sparkling white terraces of shallow limestone pools rather like the shapes of oyster shells cling precariously to the hillside. From a distance they look like piles of raw cotton, a crop that you find in fields all across this part of the country. Close up, the limestone is brilliant white and its edges glitter like diamonds.

THINGS TO SEE & DO

The Travertine Cascades

This is the place where you will find the famed cascades, where several storeys of pure white shallow bowls, filled with azure blue waters, shimmer in the sunshine.

Unfortunately, Pamukkale's popularity has also brought problems. In the early days, there was no protection for this delicate environment. People broke the sides of the pools as they climbed over them and sun oils from swimmers left a residue in the water that discoloured the white limestone. To add to the situation, several hotels that had been built above the cascade were using water directly from the spring for

HOW IT HAPPENS

The hot springs that emerge from the top of the hill in Pamukkale are rich in minerals. As the water cascades down the side of the hill, it leaves a microscopic layer of these minerals in any undulation on the ground and in the bowls of the pools. This turns white as it hardens. Over millions of years, these thin layers have built up and in some places at Pamukkale they are metres thick.

their own private swimming pools – this meant that there was not enough spring water reaching the limestone pools to repair the damage.

By the early 1990s 'cotton castle' was in real danger of ruin. As a result, in the mid-1990s, the Turkish authorities instigated an action plan to save the cascades. The hotels on the plateau have now been bulldozed and the waters are being trained over the most damaged sections to make them white once again, a bit like the teeth-whitening process that is so fashionable at the moment. People have been banned from bathing in or walking on the pools. There is a footpath that you can follow as long as you take your shoes off, but it is a bit painful for soft feet. However, all these changes have made a tremendous difference in less than ten years and the total area of white limestone is beginning to expand again.

About 300 km (186 miles) northeast of Bodrum

24 hours a day, ticket office 08.00–19.00 May–Oct; 08.00–17.00 Nov–Apr Admission charge when ticket office is open

Hierapolis

The Romans loved natural springs, which they thought could cure various ailments. Hierapolis, the city they built here on top of the plateau next to Pamukkale, was really a giant spa town. Walk down the Cardo, the colonnaded main street, to the Gate of Domitian or explore the necropolis (cemetery), with its collection of more than 1,200 tombs and giant sarcophagi. The **museum** on site displays a range of items found during excavation of the site. Extra ticket charge

Pamukkale Thermal Baths

Open since Roman times, the modern buildings have been built directly on top of the ancient ones. In fact, while bathing, you can sit on fallen Roman columns that lie just under the surface of the water. The warm springs are said to be good for a long list of ailments – although most people just come for the fun of swimming there. Even if you do not want to get wet (extra charge), come and have a look at the pools.

08.00–20.00

Aphrodisias

In ancient times, Aphrodisias was famous for its school of sculpture and art. Getting a place to study here virtually guaranteed a successful career. Because of the school, the city was one of the most beautifully decorated in the ancient world and the statues excavated here are some of the best at any ancient site in Europe.

HISTORY

Aphrodisias was founded in the 7th century BC as a centre of worship of Aphrodite, goddess of love and beauty, who gave the city its name. When a source of fine marble was discovered nearby, the school was founded and the city thrived from the 5th century BC. Unfortunately, the site was prone to earthquakes. This and the fall of the Roman Empire in the 4th century AD brought an end to the good times. People continued to live there but there was no money to repair the damaged buildings. The city was abandoned in the early 14th century to be replaced by a small rural village. Archaeologists did not get a chance to work on the site until 1956, when another earthquake forced the villagers to relocate.

THINGS TO SEE & DO

Museum

This is one site where the European archaeologists did not get the chance to take all the best stuff to their own museums back home. The collection here is stunning, probably the best museum of ancient sculpture in Turkey. Every work is of a high standard, but look particularly for the formal statue of the goddess Aphrodite carved with reliefs of the Three Graces, sun and moon god and cupid. All of these are symbols of the Aphrodite cult.

08.00–19.00 May–Oct; 08.00–17.30 Nov–Apr Admission charge

South Agora

This huge market place was planned and built in the 1st century AD and originally had two porticoes (covered walkways) of Ionic columns running 200 m (220 yds) down each flank. Some of these have been re-erected. Excavations show that the Tiberius Portico at the southern flank was decorated with highly ornate friezes and inscriptions praising Emperor Tiberius. You can see examples of these in the museum.

Stadium

The largest ancient stadium in Turkey and the best preserved in the whole Mediterranean, this is an impressive structure with a length of 262 m (287 yds) and a width of 60 m (65 yds) surrounded by well-preserved stands with a capacity of 30,000. The stadium was originally used for athletics competitions. It even held mini-Olympics-type competitions for the Asia Minor province. In the 7th century, after the theatre was damaged in an earthquake, it also held circus and wild-animal shows that were then the height of fashion.

Temple of Aphrodite

The centre of the city and its most important building, the temple was originally the centre of worship to the protector goddess of the city. Worshippers would have travelled from around Asia Minor to visit the site and this would have brought a lot of money to the area. It would have been a large and ornate structure, but only 14 of the 40 columns still remain. In the early Christian era (3rd–5th century AD) it was converted into a church and most of the ornate pagan decoration was destroyed. A large statue to the goddess was found just outside the temple precinct and this is on display in the museum.

Tetrapylon

The most beautiful of the remains discovered in the city, the tetrapylon is a monumental double archway built in the 2nd century AD at a major road junction in the city. Sixteen finely fluted Corinthian columns support a pediment of incredibly high craftsmanship.

Theatre

Hidden under a massive 40 m (131 ft) of earth until the 1970s, the theatre – semicircular in design with white marble seating – was built into a natural hill. The *cavea* and stage were added when the Hellenistic design got a facelift during the Roman era, allowing gladiatorial contests.

Tetrapylon

The Menderes Valley & Bafa Gölü (Lake Bafa)

This full-day tour links some of the Aegean's lesser-visited but equally prestigious ancient sites. Driving south from Kuşadası, this 200 km (120 mile) round trip includes the Ionian settlement of Priene, the Roman remains of Miletus and the site of the famous Oracle at Didyma. The trip ends at the wonderfully serene Bafa Gölü (Lake Bafa) where you can enjoy a simple meal of fresh fish or *meze* (see page 96) before returning to your hotel. Better still, stay to watch the sunset over the water and enjoy the buzzing of the cicadas as night falls.

To begin, leave Kuşadası on the main road south (D515), and turn left just after the town of Söke, signposted Priene (road number 09–55). The site is on the right just after the village of Güllübahçe.

THINGS TO SEE & DO

Priene

Set on a terraced hillside overlooking the Menderes Valley, the remains of Priene sit among magnificent mature fragrant pines in the lee of a rocky peak. Priene was originally founded on the valley bottom, but when its access to the sea silted up, the population moved up the hill to a new town in the 4th century BC, making Priene one of the world's first pre-planned settlements. The revolutionary layout of straight streets with intersections was designed by Hippodamus of Miletus in the 5th century BC. His theories spread through the known world and were used in the planning of modern cities like Paris and New York.

Temple of Athena The most important monument in the city is the Temple of Athena, built in the 3rd century BC with money given to the city by Alexander the Great, who stayed here in 334 BC.

Housing district The remains of hundreds of family homes can be seen on the far flank of the site (the western section), past the *agora* and *stoa*. Only the lower parts of the walls remain in place. There is a

sign that indicated the very house where Alexander was invited to stay, probably by an important town official, but there is no evidence of this inside, and the structure does not look any different from the rest.

Stoa and agora Sitting at a major intersection in the centre of Priene, the *stoa* and *agora* are built of monumental stone blocks with far less decoration than buildings found at Ephesus (see page 75) or Miletus (see below). The Romans had little influence here, especially in terms of the architectural style. The view from the remains of the *stoa* and the *agora* beyond is breathtaking. 08.30–18.30 May–Oct; 08.30–17.30 Nov–Apr Admission charge

From Priene carry on along the main road – right at the junction. After about 8 km (5 miles) there is a right turning towards Didyma (Didim). You will cross the River Menderes and see a signpost left to Miletus (Miletos).

Miletus (Miletos)

An important sea-port in ancient Greek times, Miletus was a large and very rich city. The principal port of entry to the region under the Greeks, Miletus was more important than Ephesus, but the Romans preferred Ephesus so influence shifted north. The other problem for Miletus was that it suffered even more than Ephesus from the silting up of its port. The site is now several kilometres from the sea and all this fertile farmland has been laid down in the last 1,500–2,000 years.

The theatre The largest in Turkey, this ancient theatre has not been renovated like the one at Ephesus. The *cavea* (seating area) and vaulted walkways underneath it are well preserved, allowing you to explore the structure, including chambers where the wild animals would have been kept before gladiatorial contests. Above the theatre is a small Byzantine castle with views down over the whole structure.

The rest of the city The old harbour used to be behind the theatre. Two stone lions held the chain barring ships from entering when the

harbour closed each winter. Along the marble-lined Sacred Way, which linked Miletus with Didyma, you can explore the remains of an *agora*, gymnasium and partially reconstructed Ionic *stoa*. 08.30–19.00 May–Oct; 08.30–17.30 Nov–Apr Admission charge

From Miletus rejoin the main road and continue towards the modern village of Didyma (Didim), passing through the village of Akköy as you go.

Didyma (Didim)

Perhaps the most impressive single monument on the west coast, this temple was the third-largest structure of the ancient Greek world when it was built. It was surrounded by 124 marble columns and decorated with some of the best sculptures and friezes in the empire.

Archway detail, Priene

This is the site where the Greek god Zeus came down to earth to make love to the goddess Leto, who then gave birth to twins Artemis and Apollo. Over time, the sacred spring at the site became famous throughout the ancient Greek world as the site of a powerful oracle, dedicated to Apollo.

In 494 BC the Oracle was destroyed by the Persians and the spring dried up, but it began to flow again when Alexander the Great called in for a consultation in 334 BC. The Oracle proclaimed Alexander 'Son of Zeus', which boosted his image and put the Oracle back at the top of its game.

By the 3rd century AD, Christianity had become well established in the area and the sanctuary gradually fell into disuse. In AD 385, it was officially closed on the orders of the Byzantine Emperor Theodosius.

The porch The entrance to this temple consists of a monumental staircase and an entrance porch that is one of the most complete and impressive in Turkey. Over 100 of the columns are still standing (although only three of these are to their full height) and still form a curtain around the inner chamber.

Inner Chamber Reached by two narrow, sloping tunnels, the inner sanctum was where the power of the Oracle was contained. Off limits

THE ROLE OF THE ORACLE

In the ancient world, the gods and goddesses influenced the fate of all mortals. The Oracle was said to be able to speak to these gods, and rich and influential people came to the Oracle for consultations, hoping that the gods would look favourably on them.

Of course, mortals could not talk directly to the Oracle or to the gods. That was the job of the priests or priestesses who served here. They had the secret of how to get the answers, perhaps by spells, incantations and natural hallucinogenic gases.

to everyone but the priests and priestesses, it was divided into living quarters, sacred sanctums and consulting rooms. Now it is a single large and semi-open space.

The 'Furious Medusa' An exquisite marble head adorns the steps at the entrance to the site. An emblem of the southern Aegean, its image can be found on postcards and tourist brochures. Although christened the 'furious Medusa' by local Turks, archaeologists now think that this is the god Apollo, patron of the temple. 08.00–19.00 May–Oct; 08.00–17.00 Nov–Apr Admission charge

From Didyma retrace your steps back to Akköy and then turn right, travelling through the countryside until you reach the main Kuşadası/Bodrum road. Turn right and follow the road until you reach the village of Bafa. Turn left here, signposted Kapıkırı, following the twisting road to the lakeshore 14 km (9 miles) away.

Bafa Gölü (Lake Bafa)

This brackish lake was formed when the mouth of Latmos Gulf was cut off from the sea. Today it covers over 100 sq km (39 sq miles) and is surrounded by the barren, treeless peaks of the Latmos Mountain range. Tantalising remains of Roman buildings and later Byzantine towers and churches sit on the water's edge and on small islands offshore. You can visit these on a boat trip.

Around the lake In the hills behind the lake's edge are more remains of the city of **Heracleia ad Latmos**, some of which lie side by side with the modern farming community of **Kapıkırı** (there is a ticket office for the site just before the village centre; you need to buy a ticket during the day). The village itself provides a fascinating insight into rural Turkey, with donkeys still used as transport and crops tended by hand. The women will want to sell you their handmade lace, which is a thriving cottage industry here.

Turn down to the lake's edge and you will reach a couple of small family-owned restaurants including **Selene's** (0252 543 5221).

Selçuk

The little town of Selçuk is the closest community to Ephesus, so it has been rather thrust into the spotlight in recent years. The excellent Ephesus Museum is the most important reason to visit, but the town has other historical attractions that would fill an extra couple of hours. For more information contact Selçuk tourist office ⓐ Agora Çorşışı (across from the museum) ⓣ 0232 892 6328

THINGS TO SEE & DO

Basilica of St John

If this 5th-century AD church were still complete it would be the seventh-largest cathedral in the world. Built to honour the burial site of the apostle St John the Evangelist, who settled here in the 1st century AD, the church was erected using the finest marbles and semi-precious stones. The remains of the nave wall give the best impression of how large and impressive the church would have been. If you find this hard to imagine, look at the drawing on the information panel on the site, which depicts the complete structure.

An impressive 6th-century AD castle, **Ayasoluk**, stands over the site with demanding views across the valley.

ⓐ St John Caddesi ⓑ 08.00–17.00 ⓘ Admission charge

Ephesus Museum

If you visit the site of Ephesus (see page 75) then you must also visit Ephesus Museum. This is where the best of the artefacts found at the site are on display. The museum is not too big and overwhelming. The first gallery, a re-creation of a Roman room excavated at the site, is complete with furniture and a small domestic shrine. The range of everyday objects on display is impressive, from hairpins to leather sandals. More precious objects include gold filigree jewellery and fine Samian tableware. Several rooms display monumental statuary and friezes that decorated temples and public buildings.

Room 7 is set aside for statues of the goddess Artemis, the patroness of Ephesus and goddess of fertility, but the final room is the Hall of the Emperors, where statues and busts of many Roman leaders have been brought together.

Agora Çorşısı 08.00–12.00; 13.00–19.00 (17.00 winter)

Admission charge

İsa Bey Mosque

Built in the 14th century, this is one of the oldest working mosques in the region and is worth a visit for its architectural beauty. It was built by the Seljuks, who ruled this land before the arrival of the Ottomans, but the interior is decorated in both Seljuk and Ottoman style, making it an important transitional building. Once inside, look at the column capitals that support the domes – one is a recycled Roman column, most probably taken from Ephesus.

St John Caddesi 24 hours except during prayers

Remains of the Basilica of St John

EXCURSIONS

Day trip to Kos (Greece)

The Knights of St John came here and built another castle just as impressive as the one at Bodrum, overlooking the harbour at Kos town, the capital of the island of Kos. The impressive Roman remains right in the centre of town were only discovered after an earthquake in 1933. Also visit the Hippocrates Tree – locals will tell you this is where the 'father of medicine', a native of the island, would lecture to his students over 2,500 years ago. The tree has proved to be one of the oldest in Europe, but sadly most experts believe that it is only 2,000 years old and not of Hippocrates' era.

ⓘ The crossing from Bodrum takes around 90 minutes

Meryem Ana

This is one of the most important religious sites in Turkey, and a place revered by both Christians and Muslims. Discovered in 1891, this shady spot beside a babbling brook is said to be the home and final resting place of the Virgin Mary. Known in Turkish as *Meryem Ana* (House of the Virgin Mary), the site was visited by Pope Paul VI in 1967, when he approved the site as genuine.

A simple Byzantine chapel now sits on the spot where the Madonna's house was said to have stood. The foundations of this building have been dated to the 1st century AD, which matches the date when Mary is said to have left the Holy Land after the death of Jesus.

A Mass is held every Sunday morning, and Meryem Ana is always crowded at the Feast of the Assumption on 15 August.

ⓐ Off route E87, 7 km (4 miles) south of Ephesus ⓒ dawn–dusk

ⓘ Free admission to church but parking fee/entrance to compound

---

Turkish carpets are a prized souvenir

LIFESTYLE
Aegean life

Turkish Delight and a cup of Çay

Food & drink

Turkish cuisine is considered to be one of the three greatest in the world. For an excellent book on the subject, see *Turkish Cookery* by Sally Mustoe (Saqi Books). Although the days of the great Ottoman banquets are long gone, Turks still make meal times an event.

Freshness is the key to Turkish food – you only have to look at the mountains of seasonal fruit and vegetables on sale in local markets or the seafood on ice at harbourfront restaurants. Dishes are generally cooked in olive oil and a range of herbs and spices has traditionally been used to add flavour, although these are never overpowering.

WHEN TO EAT

Turks take a very relaxed approach to mealtimes. There will always be somewhere open no matter what time you get hungry, although you will find a more lively atmosphere between 12.00 and 14.30 for lunch and between 19.00 and 22.00 for dinner, when other people head out to eat. Only the most formal restaurants close between lunch and dinner and eateries of all kinds tend to stay open until the last client leaves.

WHERE TO EAT

Look out for the following different styles of eateries – depending on your appetite:

Kahve A Turkish coffee house that does not serve food and is usually where men get together for a game of backgammon or a gossip.

Lokanta A casual, often family-owned restaurant serving a small range of home-cooked dishes. There will probably not be a printed menu, but it is normal to go into the kitchen to see what is being cooked. Point at what you want if the staff do not speak English.

Restoran A more formal restaurant than a *lokanta*. A *restoran* will have a printed menu with prices.

Kebapçı Specialises in grilled meats. They vary from pretty, family-owned establishments with outdoor terraces to small, urban kiosks.

Meyhane A bar- or pub-style place serving *meze* with drinks. Traditionally these have been for males only, but in tourist areas women will also be welcomed.

Pideci These small snack bars serve Turkish pizza.

Büfe A basic snack bar.

Pastane Turkish patisseries serving cakes and pastries.

WHAT TO EAT

Meze dishes or starters

Turks prefer to eat *meze* style. That is where several small dishes are served at once and shared by everyone around the table. Try eating *meze* style for a truly authentic experience or order these dishes as a starter.

Cold options include *yaprak dolması* (stuffed vine leaves), fresh olives, *imam bayıldı* (slices of aubergine with tomatoes and onions in olive oil) and *cacık* (a refreshing dip of natural yoghurt and cucumber with a hint of mint). Warm *meze* dishes include *börek* (filo pastry squares filled with cheese and herbs) and *midye dolması* (stuffed mussels).

Because Turks eat meze style you may find that if you order starters and main courses they will both arrive together. To avoid this, order only one course at a time.

Main courses

The most popular form of main course is grilled or barbecued meat, usually lamb, but you will also find some beef. It is grilled as chops or steak but also cubed and skewered for *şiş kepabs*, thinly sliced for *döner kepabs* or minced for *köfte* (meat balls) or *İskender kepab* (minced meat

TIPPING

Most *restoran* will add 10–15 per cent to your bill, but you should still leave a little something for the waiter. *Lokanta* will normally not add service to the bill. It is customary to leave 10–15 per cent. Leave small change on the table at bars and coffee houses.

wrapped around a skewer). Meat is always fresh and is generally served cooked through, not pink in the middle or rare.

Fresh fish is plentiful and delicious. You will find it elaborately displayed on ice at restaurant entrances. It is, however, always the most expensive item on the menu. It is sold by weight, so you choose a fish and it will be weighed and priced for you, then cooked to your specifications. If you find the price beyond your budget you get the chance to change your mind before it is too late.

You will normally find that your main meal comes with bread and salad and either rice or chips.

In Turkey, food is usually served warm rather than hot, which usually means that chips arrive soggy, not crisp. If you want yours piping hot, tell the waiter when you order.

Plenty of spices are used in Turkish cooking

Snacks

Turkey has excellent pizza (*pide*, or *lahmacun*). It is lighter than the Italian variety and often served rolled up so you can eat it on the go. Equally delicious are *döner kebaps*, slivers of lamb wrapped with salad in pitta bread, which you can find on almost every street corner. *Gözleme* are pancakes or crêpes with sweet or savoury fillings, while *simit* (bread rings sprinkled with sesame seeds) are perfect for stopping those afternoon hunger pangs.

Sweets

Turkish sweets and puddings are world renowned and make no apology for the amount of calories they contain. The most famous, *baklava* – layers of filo pastry soaked in butter, sprinkled with nuts then baked in honey syrup – is a work of art. Milk puddings are also popular, as are delicious rich rice puddings.

Lokum, or Turkish Delight (a jelly sweet traditionally flavoured with rose water but made with many fruit flavours today), makes a great accompaniment to Turkish coffee. If all this really sounds a little over the top, most *lokantas* and *restorans* offer fresh melon or other seasonal fruit as a lighter but equally delicious end to your meal. The sweet toothed will need to head to a specialist café for dessert. These are often very basic establishments with vinyl-topped tables and fluorescent lights, so they do not get points for romantic ambience, but they are full of authentic atmosphere.

International food

More and more 'international' food has become available in Turkey. This includes all-day English breakfasts if that is what you want, as well as other familiar items like pizzas and burgers. If you want to splash out, the large, upmarket hotels will have formal and expensive restaurants serving 'continental' menus with silver service.

Drinks

Bottled water, the usual array of fizzy soft drinks and international spirits are readily available, so you will certainly find something familiar during your trip.

You may want to try a particularly Turkish beverage. *Khave*, or Turkish coffee, is strong but never harsh and is served in small cups. Take it *sade* (no sugar), *az şekerli* (a little sugar) or *şekerli* (sweet), but never try to empty the cup because there are grounds in the bottom.

Çay (tea) is served weak without milk in tulip-shaped glasses. Apple tea is a refreshing alternative. Another delicious, non-alcoholic drink is *ayran*, a refreshing savoury natural yoghurt drink.

Turkey produces some excellent wine; look for the trade names *Doluca* and *Kavaklıdere* for quality and reliability. It also brews a good, clean-tasting Pilsen-type beer under the brand name *Efes*, but for something more potent try *rakı*, an anise-based spirit that is diluted with water. It is drunk both as a before- and after-dinner drink, but at a strength of 40° should always be taken in moderation.

'Cheers' in Turkish is *şerefe* (pronounced sheri-fey).

Turkish Çay (tea) is one of the most popular drinks in Turkey

Menu decoder

A FEW BASIC WORDS

Alabalık Freshwater trout

Aşure Sweet 'soup' of fruits, nuts, pulses and bulgar wheat

Balık Fish

Barbunya Red mullet

Beyti Minced kepab in pitta bread

Bonfile Steak

Börek Savoury pastry usually with cheese filling but can be meat

Bülbül yuvası (swallow's nest) Shredded wheat in sugar syrup

Çay Tea

Çöp kebap Finely chopped meat or offal

Dolma Vine leaves stuffed with rice and herbs

Döner kebap Thin slices of grilled lamb sliced from a cone of meat

Ekmek Bread

Fasulye Haricot beans in tomato sauce

Fırında sütlaç Oven-baked rice pudding, usually served cold

Gözleme A wafer-thin crepe with sweet or savoury filling

Güllaç Flaky pastry and milk flavoured with nuts and rose water

Güveç Meat and/or vegetable stew, cooked in a clay pot

Hamsi Anchovies

Haydari Yoghurt dip flavoured with garlic

Imam bayıldı Baked aubergine with tomatoes and onions served cold

İskander kebap Minced meat cooked around a skewer and served in yoghurt or tomato sauce

Istakoz Lobster

Kabak tatlısı Baked squash topped with clotted cream (*kaymak*)

Kahve Turkish coffee

Kalamar Squid

Karides Shrimp

Karısık ızgara Mixed grill of lamb meat

Karnıyarık Aubergines stuffed with minced lamb, currants and pine nuts then baked

Karpuz Watermelon
Kayısı Apricot
Kiraz Cherry
Kuzu Lamb
Lahmacun A wafer-thin pizza topped with tomato sauce and minced lamb
Levrek Sea bass
Maden suyu Mineral water
Mantı Noodle dough ravioli parcels filled with meat
Menemen Stir-fried omelette with hot peppers and vegetables
Mercimek çorbası Lentil soup
Midye Mussel
Pastırma Dry-cured beef served thinly sliced
Pide Small, flat pizzas with a thin topping of minced lamb or cheese
Pilav Rice
Piliç Roast chicken
Pirzola Lamb chops
Piyaz Haricot beans in vinaigrette
Portakal Orange
Salata Salad
Şarap Wine
Sardalya Sardine
Sığır Beef
Şiş kebap Cubes of meat put on a skewer then grilled
Su Water
Süt Milk
Tarama Pink fish-roe paste
Tavuk Boiled chicken
Tel kadayıf Shredded wheat base smothered in honey syrup and chopped nuts
Turşu Pickled vegetables
Tuz Salt
Yayla çorbası Rice soup
Yoğurt çorbası Yoghurt soup

Shopping

Shopping in Aegean Turkey offers something for everyone, with a whole range of excellent souvenirs in all price brackets. You will be bombarded with designer 'rip-offs' offering those 'must-have names' at a fraction of the price back home. Stock up on items by your favourite fashion house but check merchandise carefully as quality varies from good to terrible.

Leather is one of the top ten buys for tourists. You will find a fantastic range of bags, belts and jackets. Again, designer names predominate but you can find traditional styles or have something made just for you.

Turkey is famous for its handicrafts and these include inlaid wooden items like small tables or chess sets, copper pots, rustic ceramics and pottery, onyx or pipes carved from meerschaum, a soft, white clay-like material found only in Turkey.

Gold and silver jewellery is also good value since items such as chains and bracelets are priced by weight. You can have things made at small jewellery workshops within a few days. Gold is usually 14-carat quality. Always check for the hallmark on gold and silver items.

The prize souvenir has to be the handmade Turkish carpet. These have been woven for centuries, and each region has traditional patterns and colours. The best are made of silk but most are of wool.

Kilims are different from carpets because they have a flat weave rather than a pile. They are just as colourful but generally cheaper and they make great rugs and throws.

BROWSING

Browsing and window shopping are not something that the Turks do. When a shopkeeper sees you looking at his wares he assumes you have an interest in buying. They would rather you buy from them than the shop next door so they will put a lot of effort into getting you to stop, look and try.

BARTERING

Bartering or bargaining is a fact of life in Turkey. It is not something that comes naturally to a shopper who is used to fixed prices, but that does not mean that it is something to be nervous about. If you are in the market to buy an expensive souvenir, you will be paying well over the odds if you simply pay what the shopkeeper asks. There are several tips to make the bartering process more successful and enjoyable.

To start with, act cool about the specific item you want. Look at several items and then perhaps tell the shopkeeper you want to look in other shops to compare goods. You will be offered a drink – Turkish tea or a soft drink – and it shows that you are more serious about buying if you accept. Your first offer should be around 50 per cent, or half what the shop owner is asking, then increase your offer little by little. You will probably end up paying around 70 per cent of the original asking price, but early or late in the season it could be more. If you do not want to pay the price, simply tell the shop owner and walk away. He may call you back with a lower offer. Once you agree a price it is very bad manners to change your mind.

You will get a better price if you pay in cash not by credit card and better still if you pay in UK pounds or euros than in Turkish Lira.

Turkish carpets are world famous and worth seeking out

Children

Turkey is an ideal destination for children. The simple pleasures of guaranteed sunshine, excellent beaches and warm water to play in will keep them happy for hours. Add to this the child-friendly environment, where children are welcomed in restaurants and cafés, and it makes for a very relaxed holiday. Exuberance is not frowned upon here. Turks love children and allow them the freedom to enjoy their childhood.

That said, you will find fewer attractions specifically aimed at children than in many European destinations. There are no children's museums, few 'theme' parks and no games arcades. But the jet skiing and water rides make up for that, as well as the chance to spot a wild dolphin or turtle during a boat trip.

TIPS FOR A CHILD-FRIENDLY TRIP

Turkish excursions can be 'history' heavy and even some adults can tire of this. Pace the sightseeing so that you can alternate days of gazing at

The beach at Altinkum is lovely for children

ancient buildings and tramping ancient streets with days by the pool or on the beach.

An afternoon siesta will help young children stay up late with the Turkish children – who are often still eating ice cream and playing in town squares until midnight. Early afternoon is also a good time to hide from the sun (see below).

BEACHES & ACTIVITIES

The best beaches in the region for children are the shallows of the southern Çeşme peninsula – Altınkum and Alaçatı (see pages 16 and 21) – as well as the good facilities of Ladies Beach and Pamucak at Kuşadası (see page 27), and the fine sand of Bitez (see page 55) or Gümbet close to Bodrum (see page 49).

All these offer a good range of watersports, which will suit active older children. They can take windsurfing lessons if they want to or just enjoy an exhilarating banana ride. For a gentler time it is possible to rent kayaks to explore the coastal shallows. Be aware that the winds around the Çeşme peninsula can be strong, so keep inexperienced windsurfers and kayakers under supervision. Kuşadası also has three large and modern water parks with rides for children of all ages, including safe areas for very young children.

On a totally different subject, the castles at Çeşme (see page 18) and Bodrum (see page 40) offer a chance for imaginations to run wild. Think 'swashbuckling' or 'Pirates of the Caribbean' and you have the idea.

TAKE CARE IN THE SUN

The Turkish sun is very hot and can damage young skin easily. Always make sure that children wear a high-factor sun cream. Reapply regularly and especially after they have been in the water. Limit children's time in the sun, especially from midday through the early afternoon, when the sun is at its strongest. Make sure they wear a hat and always carry a lightweight but long-sleeved garment for them in case their shoulders and arms need covering up. Keep children well hydrated – they may not complain of feeling thirsty, but will need lots of liquid to keep them well.

Sports & activities

BOAT TRIPS

A huge flotilla of boats offers day trips and these are good value for money, with lunch and drinks included. It could be to a remote beach or a historic site, but all offer delightful panoramic views of the Turkish coastline and a chance to spot a dolphin or a turtle.

It pays to do a little research and price comparison. Check out what is included in the price before making a decision. Tickets usually need to be booked the day before.

CLIMBING

The Kaynaklar climbing area just outside Kaynaklar village is 45 km (28 miles) southeast of İzmir. There are set routes for experienced climbers, but no instruction, so it is not recommended for beginners.

SCUBA DIVING

The warm, clear waters around the Turkish coast make for great diving, but because of the many ancient remains lying in the coastal shallows, numerous locations remain off limits and divers must be accompanied by a registered Turkish guide or dive master. If you are already qualified, bring your certification with you in order to book a guide.

If you want to learn to dive, most large resorts have schools that are accredited by a Professional Association of Diving Instructors (PADI), where you can be assured of good-quality training.

Many schools also offer taster sessions for people who have never dived before. After some instruction you will be allowed to do a dive under strict supervision – this is a great introduction to the sport.

WATERSPORTS

You will not be short of watersports unless you choose a particularly quiet resort. From jet skiing to banana boat rides there is something for all the family.

Wakeboarders enjoy the Aegean waters around Turkey

WINDSURFING

The Aegean coast benefits from perfect wind conditions with a prevailing north/south offshore breeze. Expert windsurfers and wakeboarders flock to two centres of excellence, Alaçatı close to Çeşme (see page 15), and Bitez near Bodrum (see page 55), both of which hold international competitions. This is also a great place for beginners and improvers, with high-calibre instruction at both centres. All along the coast there are small schools offering lessons and board rentals.

YACHTING

Touring Turkey on a boat-based rather than a hotel-based package holiday is a popular and easy option. The most famous itinerary is **The Blue Voyage** (see page 44), but British-based holiday companies offer several different routes for one- or two-week stays. See
Ⓦ www.sunsail.co.uk, Ⓦ www.moorings.co.uk or
Ⓦ www.yachtingturkey.com for more details.

If you do not want to spend your whole holiday at sea, try renting a boat, or a *gület* (a traditional wooden boat), for a day to sail off and find your own private cove or deserted beach. You can rent a boat with a crew at most marinas for a daily fee with lunch included. Although it is far more expensive than taking one of the many commercial boat tours, it is still much better value than in other parts of the Mediterranean.

Festivals & events

Turkey's festivals and events reflect its fascinating and unique society. A secular republic, it is very proud of its fight for independence, marking the major events with great solemnity. However, over 90 per cent of Turkey's population are Muslim, so they also celebrate the main Islamic festivals, especially in the countryside. On top of this, Turkey holds a whole host of sporting competitions and folk festivals.

CIVIL CELEBRATIONS

23 April National Sovereignty and Children's Day celebrates the establishment of the first Grand National Assembly in 1920, which saw the end of the Ottoman Empire.

19 May Atatürk Day and Youth and Sports Day marks the beginning of the Turkish War of Independence in 1919, when Atatürk rallied the country to fight the forces who had divided Turkish territory after World War I.

30 August Victory Day celebrates the success of Turkish forces over the Greek army in 1922.

29 October Republic Day marks the date when the present Turkish Republic was declared in 1923.

10 November Atatürk's Death: although not a holiday, Turks mark the day of Atatürk's death in a very poignant way. At 09.05 on 10 November, the exact time of his death, the whole country comes to a standstill for a minute of silent remembrance.

MAJOR MUSLIM CELEBRATIONS

The Muslim calendar runs on a lunar cycle different from that of our solar Gregorian calendar. These celebrations change date each year.

Ramadan (Ramazan)

For the entire ninth month (30 days) of the Muslim year, Muslims fast between dawn and dusk. This marks the time when Mohammed wandered in the desert and Allah (God) revealed the verses of the Koran to him. Muslims devote Ramazan to prayer, reflection and charity.

Şeker Bayramı (She-ker Bay-ramer or the Sugar Festival)

This three-day festival celebrates the end of Ramadan. Families party together enjoying traditional foods, particularly sugary foods such as *baklava*, pastries and *lokum*.

Kurban Bayramı

The festival that commemorates the Prophet Abraham offering his son Isaac to Allah (when Allah accepted the sacrifice of a sheep instead). It takes place during the tenth month of the Muslim year.

Other Muslim festivals

Other major and minor festivals are not necessarily holidays but are the times for special prayers and family get-togethers, including:
Aşure Günü (ah-shoo-reh gew-new) The tenth day of the Islamic lunar month of Muharrem commemorates Adam repenting his sin, the birth of the Prophet Abraham, Jonah's deliverance from the whale and the martyrdom of Islamic hero Hüseyin. Also, Turks celebrate Noah's ark coming to rest on dry land.
Mevlid-i Nebi (mehv-leed ee neh-bee) The Prophet Mohammed's birthday is celebrated with mosque illuminations and special foods.

Three other days of celebration where mosques are decorated and lit up are: **Regaib Kandili**, the 'Beginning of the Three Moons'; **Berat Kandili**, the 'Day of Forgiveness'; and **Mirac Kandili**, celebrating the Prophet Mohammed's ascent into heaven.

OTHER MAJOR EVENTS IN THE AEGEAN REGION

January
Camel-wrestling Festival, Selçuk

April–May
Festival of Cinema, İzmir

June
Festival of Water Sports, Foça
Surf and Sound Sport and Music Festival, Alaçatı
Turkish Windsurf Championship, Alaçatı

June–July
International Music Festival at İzmir – performances also at Ephesus

July
Çeşme hosts an annual **International Song Contest**

August
Music and Folklore Festival, Ephesus
Triathlon, Çeşme

September
Liberation Day (9 Sept), İzmir – when the Greek Army was ousted from the city in 1922
International Festival of Culture and Art, Bodrum – events are held along Neyzen Tevfik Caddesi and in the castle compound

October
The Bodrum Cup – professional yachting competitions

Ruins of Celcus library in Ephesus

PRACTICAL INFORMATION
Tips & advice

Accommodation

Prices for a double room, usually including breakfast
£ = under £45 **££** = £45–60 **£££** = over £60

ALAÇATI (ÇEŞME)

TaşOtel £££ A lovely old building and each of the seven bedrooms has modern comforts. Breakfast in a walled garden by olive trees and a small pool. ⓐ 132 Kemalpaşa Caddesi ⓣ 0232 716 7772 ⓦ www.tasotel.com

KUŞADASI

Atamis Onura £–££ A tower block hotel outside the city centre; well managed and well versed in taking care of holidaymakers. ⓐ 140 Yavansu ⓣ 0256 622 0505 ⓦ www.onura.com

Derici ££ On the beachfront but not all the rooms face the sea; though the swimming pool, on the seventh floor, does command a grand view of the Aegean. ⓐ Atatürk Bulvarı 40 ⓣ 0256 614 8222 ⓦ www.dericihotel.com

Villa Konak ££–£££ Peaceful setting in an old building surrounded by greenery. Friendly management and above-average restaurant. ⓐ Yıdırım Caddesi 55 ⓣ 0256 612 2170 ⓦ www.villakonakhotel.com

BODRUM

Su Hotel ££–£££ At the western end of the town centre near the harbour. Worth trying to reserve a room with its own balcony and overlooking the courtyard. ⓐ Turgutreis Caddesi ⓣ 0252 316 6906 ⓦ www.suhotel.com

Golden Key £££ A boutique-style hotel close to the town centre and facing the sea. Boasts a good restaurant and a reputation for excellent service. ⓐ Şalvarağa Sokak 18 ⓣ 0252 313 0304 ⓦ www.goldenkeyhotels.com

BODRUM PENINSULA

Hotel Ambrosia £££ A stylish hotel eschewing fancy details in favour of straight lines and a modish monotone. One of the best hotels on the peninsula. ⓐ Bitez Beach ⓣ 0252 343 1886

İZMIR

Güzel İzmir ££ Middle-of-the-road hotel with 40 rooms in the city centre; fine for a one-night stay. ⓐ Eylül Meydanı Sokak 8 ⓣ 0232 484 6693 ⓦ www.guzelizmirhotel.com

Imperial £ Situated close to the main railway station, this is the best budget accommodation in İzmir. The rooms have air conditioning and their own bathrooms. ⓐ 1296 Sokak 54, Basmane ⓣ 0232 484 9771 ⓕ 0232 425 6883

Anemon £££ Part of one of Turkey's best hotel chains, the Anemon in İzmir is within walking distance of the town centre. There is an above-average breakfast buffet and free pick-up from the airport. ⓐ Mürselpaşa Bulvarı 40 ⓣ 0232 336 3656 ⓦ www.anemonhotels.com

EPHESUS/SELÇUK

Artemis Guest House £ Ideal for an overnight stay close to Ephesus, the neat rooms have their own bathrooms. There is also a laundry, kitchen and small pool. ⓐ 1012 Sokak 2 ⓣ 0232 892 1982 ⓦ www.artemisguest-house.com

Nazhan £–££ A small, well-run family hotel in an attractive setting. There is a small pool and a lovely terrace on the roof for meals and drinks. ⓐ 1044 Sokak 2 ⓣ 0232 892 8731 ⓔ nazhan@superonline.com

Kalehan ££ Furnished throughout in an elegant Ottoman style, this is a delightful stay if visiting Ephesus. There is a pool and good meals are served. ⓐ İzmir Cadessi ⓣ 0232 892 6154 ⓦ www.kalehan.com ❗ Limited number of rooms so book well in advance

Preparing to go

GETTING THERE

Turkey is a popular destination and features in the brochures of all the major package tour operators with a range of hotels and holidays in all price brackets. Prices are highest when demand is high, such as during school holiday periods, when it is wise to book as early as possible, especially of you have children.

If you are more flexible, it will be less busy and cheaper to travel early (May/June) or late in the season (September/October), when last-minute bargains are possible. Teletext, the Internet or travel agents offer ways to compare prices and facilities whatever time of year you want to travel. If you want to organise your own package you can book a scheduled flight (flexible dates) or charter flight (fixed dates of one or two weeks' duration) and find your own accommodation. Many hotels have their own websites that allow you to make and confirm booking, or use specialist companies such as **Expedia** (Ⓦ www.expedia.co.uk), **Travelocity** (Ⓦ www.travelocity.co.uk) or **Priceline** (Ⓦ www.priceline.co.uk).

You should also check the travel supplements of the weekend newspapers such as the *Sunday Telegraph* and *Sunday Times*. They often carry adverts for inexpensive flights and privately owned villas and apartments to rent.

By air

You have the choice of two airports when you travel to the Turkish Aegean. Both **İzmir Adnan Menderes International** in the north and **Bodrum/Milas** in the south take charter flights from many UK airports during the holiday season (April–October).

Sun Express (Ⓣ 01850 5959590 Ⓦ www.sun-express.co.uk) is a scheduled, low-cost airline serving the west coast of Turkey. A reliable and well-established company, Sun Express flies direct to İzmir from London (flight time 3 hrs 45 mins).

Both airports have duty-free shops, exchange bureaux, car-rental offices and taxis, but services are limited if you arrive or depart at night.

Many people are aware that air travel emits CO_2, which contributes to climate change. You may be interested in the possibility of lessening the environmental impact of your flight through the charity Climate Care, which offsets your CO_2 by funding environmental projects around the world. Visit ⓦ www.climatecare.org

TOURISM AUTHORITY

For more information about Turkey before you leave, contact the **Turkish Culture and Tourism Office** (ⓐ 4th Floor, 29–30 St James's Street, London SW1A 1HB ⓣ 020 7839 7778 ⓕ 020 7925 1388 ⓦ www.gototurkey.co.uk).

BEFORE YOU LEAVE

Holidays are supposed to be relaxing, so take a little time and plan ahead. You do not need inoculations to travel to Turkey but it would be wise to make sure that your family is up to date with shots like tetanus. It is also worth having a dental check-up before you go.

It is sensible to carry a small first-aid kit with items such as painkillers, treatment for upset stomachs, travel/sea-sickness tablets, plasters, antiseptic ointment and insect repellent. Sun cream is more expensive in Turkey, so buy this before you go. If you take any prescription medication make sure you have enough for the duration of your holiday.

ENTRY FORMALITIES

For first-time travellers, airport procedures and security can be a little intimidating but the process is simple and straightforward.

Check-in desks usually open two or three hours before a flight is scheduled to leave. Leave the house so that you arrive early at the airport. This will give you a good choice of seat and help avoid any unforeseen delay en route that will make you miss your flight. Most airports have good restaurant and café facilities and it is better to wait in them for your flight time rather than to worry about being late. You can always use this time to read up on your holiday destination.

Because Turkey is outside the EU you will be allowed to purchase goods 'duty free'. You will not be allowed to take more than the following amounts of duty-free goods into Turkey:

- 200 cigarettes or 50 cigars or 200g of tobacco
- 5 litres (9 pt) of alcohol

Documents

The most important documents you will need are tickets and passports. Make sure that passports for all members of the family are up to date. Children already named on a parent's passport can travel without their own passports, but any recent additions to the family or children not on a passport already will need to have their own. These can take up to 28 days to be issued by the passport office, although you can pay more for a quicker service. If your passport has less than three months to run on the date you arrive in Turkey, you need to renew it before you go. For further information on how to renew you passport and for current processing times, get in touch with the **Passport Agency** (t 0870 521 0410 or w www.ukpa.gov.uk). When your tickets arrive from the travel agent check that all the names, dates and times are correct.

Keep passports and travel tickets or confirmations in a safe place. If possible keep photocopies of your passport numbers and ticket information (and traveller's cheques if you take them) separately.

If you are going to hire a car while in Turkey all named drivers need to have their driver's licences with them.

MONEY

Consider changing a small amount of currency before you leave, especially if your flight arrives late in the evening or early in the morning. You can do this at a post office, travel agent (allow two or three days for the money to arrive) or at the airport just before you fly. Make sure that your credit and debit cards are up to date before you travel.

ATMs These are widespread in the resort areas. You can obtain cash with either your Maestro Card or credit card provided you have a Personal

Identification Number (PIN). Your bank or credit card company may charge more for this service.

Changing money Banks can be found in all major towns. There are plenty of exchange bureaux in resorts. Before you change money check the exchange and commission rates. You will find cashpoints (ATMs) in the larger resorts, and there are ATMs at all the airports. You can often pay in pounds rather than in Turkish Lira, so it pays to take some British cash; remember to keep this secure.

Credit cards These are becoming more widely accepted in shops and restaurants but not in cheaper *lokantas* and *pide* stalls or in the markets, so do not rely on this as your only method of payment.

Currency In January 2005, the Yeni (New) Turkish Lira or YTL replaced the old Turkish Lira, and each new Lira is worth 1,000,000 old Lira. Yeni Lira come in note denominations of 1, 5, 10, 20, 50 and 100 Lira. Each Yeni Lira is made up of 100 Kuruş, which come in coins of 1, 5, 10, 25 and 50 Kuruş. There is also a 1 Lira coin.

Traveller's cheques These provide the safest way to carry money, since they can be replaced if lost or stolen (remember to note down the cheque numbers in the event of needing to have them replaced). However, it is not always easy to find places that will accept them, and a steep commission is usually charged.

CLIMATE

The coastal areas of western Turkey have a Mediterranean climate. This means long, hot dry summers, mild winters with some rain and short, warm springs and autumns.

Average daytime temperatures are: April 20°C (68°F); May 24°C (75°F); June 29°C (84°F); July 31°C (88°F); August 32°C (90°F); September 29°C (84°F); October 24°C (75°F).

In summer you will only need light clothing – breathable and natural fabrics are best – but take lightweight trousers and a long-sleeved shirt to cover your arms and legs in case you get sunburnt.

Early or late in the season take a warmer layer like a light fleece just in case it gets a bit chilly in the evenings.

BAGGAGE ALLOWANCE

Baggage allowances are becoming more strict and the price of excess baggage (that over the amount allowed as part of your ticket) is expensive. Currently scheduled flights allow 20 kg (44 lb) of checked-in baggage (bags that go into the hold) per passenger, but charter flights have lower limits, as little as 15 kg (33 lb) for clients who have booked at the last minute or bought a flight-only package. Your tour company will tell you your limit and it will be printed on your ticket. Each passenger is also allowed to carry a small bag (5 kg/11 lb) onto the plane, plus duty-free shopping and items such as laptop computers or cameras.

If you think you may want to take more than this allowance, ask about buying extra baggage capacity before you travel (preferably at the same time as you book your ticket). Many airlines can sell extra capacity to you that will be much less expensive than would be the case if you just turned up at the check-in desk with overweight bags.

If you are going to be travelling with a large item – a pushchair, golf clubs or surfboard, for example – let the holiday company know when you make the booking. There may be an extra charge for these.

The prices of some items, such as spirits and cigarettes, can be less expensive in Turkey than in the duty-free shops at the airport.

During your stay

AIRPORTS

There is good road access to the region's airports, but if you are returning a rental car at the end of your holiday allow plenty of time to reach the airport and check in for your flight. If your flight departs at night the airport will have limited facilities during your wait so it might be wise to take drinks and snacks. Also, duty-free shops may not be open at night.

Book airport parking or overnight accommodation close to the airport as soon as you have booked your holiday. Demand for both is high, especially in the summer. Some hotels offer free parking for a one- or two-week holiday if you book rooms with them.

COMMUNICATIONS

Most resorts have modern public phone boxes that offer international direct dialling to the UK. Phone boxes operate with major credit cards or phone cards that can be purchased at press kiosks, tourist offices and post offices. Your personal portable phone should also work, although the cost of calls is a lot higher than at home. Check this out with your service provider before you leave. Most upmarket and resort hotels offer international direct dialling that allows you to phone home from your room.
Hotels often charge a high premium; ask about rates in advance.

Post Post offices have yellow signs with the black letters PTT. Most are open government office hours and offer postal and telecommunications services. Shops selling postcards may also sell stamps. A postcard to Europe or the US costs 0.80 Lira and will take up to a week to arrive.

CUSTOMS

There are no local customs that visitors should be especially aware of because in coastal resort areas Turkish people have become very accustomed to overseas visitors. Turkey, though, is generally a conservative country and excessive behaviour of any kind is frowned upon.

DRESS CODES

Beachwear is best kept to the beach; nude bathing is not acceptable. Restaurants do not have dress codes, but smart-casual attire is appropriate for an evening meal in a non-buffet restaurant.

ELECTRICITY

Power is 220 volts (50 Hz). Plugs are European style with two round pins so you will need an adaptor for your electrical appliances.

EMERGENCY TELEPHONE NUMBERS

Police 155
Ambulance 112
Fire 110

GETTING AROUND

Car hire The easiest way to rent a car is to book it on the internet at the same time as you book your holiday. A good and reliable Turkish company to use is **Decar** (Ⓦ www.decar.com) with a pick-up at the airport. An up-to-date map of the Aegean coast is available from **Roger Lascelles** (Ⓦ www.rogerlascellesmaps.co.uk).

You will need to leave a deposit and show your driving licence. For all car rentals, make sure you get a contact telephone number in case you have mechanical problems. Drivers must be over 21 years of age (some companies 25 years) and have held a full licence for at least a year.

Driving In Turkey you drive on the right and overtake on the left (the opposite of the UK). Speed limits are 50km/h (31 mph) in urban areas, 90 km/h (56 mph) on main roads and 120 km/h (75 mph) on motorways and dual carriageways – unless the signs indicate another limit. Seat belts are compulsory in front seats and back seats where fitted.

The main coast road and other major roads are generally in good condition, but small roads vary in quality and some are dirt surface rather than asphalt.

TELEPHONING TURKEY

To call Turkey from the UK, dial 00 90 followed by the area code (minus the initial 0), then the 7-digit number.

TELEPHONING ABROAD

To call an overseas number from Turkey, dial 00 followed by the country code (UK=44) and the area code (minus the initial 0), then the rest of the number.

You will meet all kinds of traffic on the roads, from large, modern trucks to donkey and carts (and the occasional loose farm animal). You will need to be on the alert for slower-moving vehicles. Slower traffic will usually move onto the hard shoulder to allow you to pass.

If Turkish drivers want to cross the traffic, they will often pull over to the right and let traffic behind them pass before making the turn so they do not hold everyone up.

When traffic is quieter (at night and on Sundays), Turkish traffic lights are switched to flashing amber. This means that you will need to pay attention because there is a junction or crossroads ahead that is not controlled.

Parking is a problem in all the major resorts. Do not park where you see a yellow kerb.

You will find both leaded and unleaded petrol. Not all fuel stations are self-service. A member of staff may come and clean your windscreen. This is at no extra cost, but staff will appreciate a small tip. Some petrol stations do not accept credit cards.

Public transport Long-distance bus services – all Turkish towns and cities are served by an efficient, modern and cheap bus network that makes an excellent framework for touring. Services feature air conditioning, videos (in Turkish, of course), refreshments and programmed stops for meals.

Local buses The *dolmuş* is the lifeblood of local transport. These small mini-vans run set routes, leaving the terminus when full and picking up passengers anywhere along the route. There will usually be a service from town to the main beaches and resort hotels. They are cheap and efficient.

HEALTH, SAFETY & CRIME

Should you require medical help, most hotels will have a doctor on call but you will be charged for the consultation (you can usually claim this back from your holiday insurance policy).

Hospital If you need to stay in hospital there are clean, though limited, facilities in most large towns, smaller clinics in smaller towns. Staff are well trained and most doctors can speak some English. You have to pay for treatment but depending on circumstances this could be organised directly through your insurance company. If you have travelled on a package holiday with a major tour company, your resort representative will be able to offer advice and help.

Pharmacies (Eczane) Pharmacists in Turkey are highly qualified and most will speak some English. They will be able to advise you on treatments for complaints such as minor sunburn, upset tummy, insect bites and diarrhoea. Normal opening hours are 09.00–19.00 and there will be a duty pharmacist available in every town.

Water Although tap water is clean, only drink bottled or boiled water.

Safety & crime Standards of personal safety are high and the observance of sensible precautions should ensure a trouble-free holiday. You are very unlikely to be the victim of a crime but if you do need to make a police report your hotel will be able to help.

MEDIA

The only English-language newspaper printed in Turkey is the *Turkish Daily News*. The popular English tabloids are widely available in all the leading resorts at a price premium, though they may be a day old. Most upmarket hotels will offer BBC *News 24* as part of their programming. Resort bars will often transmit Premier League matches live, and show English news reports. You will find Internet cafés in most resorts.

OPENING HOURS

Banks 08.30–12.00 & 13.30–17.00 Mon–Fri

Shops 09.00–19.00 Mon–Sat; tourist shops daily 09.00–22.00 in the resorts in summer

Government offices 08.30–12.30 & 13.30–17.30 Mon–Fri

State museums 08.30–17.30 Tues–Sun; closed for lunch in winter

Archaeological sites 08.00–18.00 or 19.00 in summer

Warning Opening hours for museums and archaeological sites change all the time. It is probably best not to arrive too early or too late at a site in case the ticket office is closed.

RELIGION

Turkey is a predominantly Muslim country although it is one of the most liberal Islamic populations in the world. Alcohol and gambling are allowed. The countryside is generally more conservative than the coastal resorts. If you are travelling away from the coast, or wanting to visit mosques or churches, modest dress is appropriate.

SMOKING

The Turkish parliament has passed a ban on smoking in public places, which is due to come into effect in 2010. However, existing partial bans are widely flouted and some anticipate that many people will flout the new law.

TIME DIFFERENCES

Turkey is two hours ahead of Greenwich Mean Time (GMT).

TIPPING

In restaurants, it is advisable to leave 10–15 per cent of the bill, plus small change for the waiter. In cafés and bars, leave a tip of small change. Bell-boys should receive 50 Kuru per bag, room cleaners should be left 50 Kuru per day, and shoe guardians in mosques welcome a small tip.

TOILETS

There are few public toilet facilities in Turkey. The best policy is to stop at a café or bar. If in a resort, visit the nearest hotel. Always carry a supply of toilet roll or tissue, as few toilets outside the hotels will have any. In museums and archaeological sites you may have to pay a small amount for use of the facilities. Keep small change handy for this.

TRAVELLERS WITH DISABILITIES

Turkey is working hard to improve facilities for the disabled but provision is still patchy. Many newly built hotels and public buildings have facilities but access to archaeological sites and historic buildings is difficult and the lack of curb ramps and controlled street crossings in towns makes movement problematical. If necessary, contact the hotels direct to ensure that they can provide what you need. For further help, contact **Holiday Care International** ⓐ 7th Floor, Sunley House, 4 Bedford Park, Croydon, Surrey CR0 2AP ⓣ 0845 124 9971 ⓦ www.holidaycare.org.uk

FIND THE LATEST HOTSPOT

Get more from your holiday and find out the best restaurants, bars, beaches and family-friendly attractions from our handy pocket guides. Our wide range covers up to 45 destinations:

- Algarve
- Bali
- Bulgaria
- Corfu
- Corsica
- Costa Blanca
- Costa Brava & Costa Dorada
- Costa del Sol & Costa de Almeria
- Côte D'Azur
- Crete
- Croatia
- Cuba
- Cyprus
- Dominican Republic
- Egypt
- Fuerteventura
- Gibraltar
- Goa
- Gran Canaria
- Guernsey
- Ibiza
- Ionian Islands
- Jamaica
- Jersey
- Lanzarote
- Madeira
- Mallorca
- Malta
- Menorca
- Mexico
- Morocco
- Neapolitan Riviera
- Orlando
- Rhodes & Kos
- Santorini
- Sardinia
- Sicily
- Sri Lanka
- Tenerife
- Thailand
- Tunisia
- Turkey –
  - Aegean Coast
  - Lycian Coast
  - Mediterranean Coast

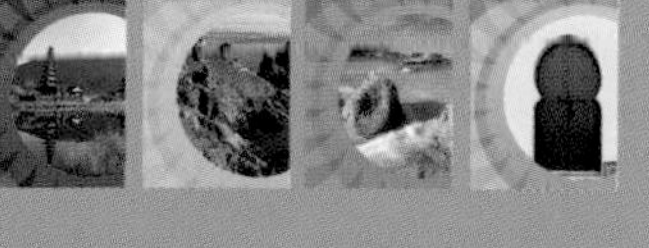

Available from all good bookshops, your local Thomas Cook travel store or browse and buy on-line at www.thomascookpublishing.com

ACKNOWLEDGEMENTS

We would like to thank all the photographers, picture libraries and organisations for the loan of the photographs reproduced in this book, to whom copyright in the photograph belongs:

Henry G. Beeker/TIPS Images page 97; Michele Burgess/SuperStock page 68; Richard Clark/BigStockPhoto.com page 107; Steve Estvanik/Dreamstime.com page 84; Jale Evsen/BigStockPhoto.com page 78; age fotostock/SuperStock page 70; Philip Gray/Dreamstime.com page 77; John McLelland/BigStockPhoto.com page 75; Pictures Colour Library pages 93, 104; Sean Sheehan pages 62, 87; Thomas Cook Tour Operations pages 5, 13, 15, 17, 39, 42, 54, 59, 65, 91, 94, 103, 111; Bertil Videt/Wikimedia Commons page 99; Wikimedia Commons page 10; World Pictures pages 1, 37, 45, 53

Project editor: Alison Coupe
Layout: Donna Pedley
Proofreader: Jan McCann
Indexer: Amanda Jones

Send your thoughts to
books@thomascook.com

- **Found a beach bar, peaceful stretch of sand or must-see sight that we don't feature?**
- **Like to tip us off about any information that needs a little updating?**
- **Want to tell us what you love about this handy little guidebook and more importantly how we can make it even handier?**

Then here's your chance to tell all! Send us ideas, discoveries and recommendations today and then look out for your valuable input in the next edition of this title.

Send an email to the above address or write to:
HotSpots Project Editor, Thomas Cook Publishing, PO Box 227, Coningsby Road, Peterborough PE3 8SB, UK